BE ONE

BE ONE

"WASTE NO MORE TIME ARGUING ABOUT WHAT A GOOD MAN SHOULD BE. **BE ONE.**"

– MARCUS AURELIUS

HOW TO BE A HEALTHY MAN IN *TOXIC TIMES*

JIMMY REX

FOREWORD BY *ED MYLETT*

WILEY

For general information on our other products and services or for technical support, please contact our Customer Care Department within the United States at (800) 762-2974, outside the United States at (317) 572-3993 or fax (317) 572-4002.

Wiley also publishes its books in a variety of electronic formats. Some content that appears in print may not be available in electronic formats. For more information about Wiley products, visit our web site at www.wiley.com.

Library of Congress Cataloging-in-Publication Data is Available:

ISBN 9781394229123 (Cloth)
ISBN 9781394229130 (ePub)
ISBN 9781394229147 (ePDF)

Cover Design: Brett Horrocks & Kesia Nielsen

SKY10064418_011124

Dedicated to the men who took a chance on me and a chance on themselves. Men committed to becoming more. The men of We Are The They.

Contents

Foreword

OVER THE YEARS, I've had the honor of coaching many remarkable individuals. I've seen countless success stories unfold before me, but what I've witnessed with Jimmy, as his mentor and friend, has been nothing short of extraordinary. He embodies the success that's entirely achievable when one approaches life with the correct mindset and leads with the heart.

BE ONE: *How to Be a Healthy Man in Toxic Times* is not just another self-help book. This is a guidebook for an entire generation of men, and those who love them, who are striving for greatness but find themselves struggling to deal with cultural pressure, societal expectations, and personal challenges. Jimmy understands the complexities of being a man in today's world and refuses to succumb to anything that will take him out of integrity. This book will teach you to do the same—to dig deep, find the best version of yourself, and unleash the power within you.

Each chapter isn't just for momentary motivation or to give you insights you've already thought of—they cover 12 core areas of your life that you can shift out of toxicity and into life-giving vitality.

I've witnessed firsthand the power of Jimmy's system and his movement, We Are The They. It's one that every man, woman, and teenager can benefit from.

So, "Why now? Why this book? Why Jimmy's system?" The answer is simple: because it works. It's real, it's raw, and it's relevant. We are living in unprecedented times, and this requires an unprecedented approach. There is an epidemic of confusion leaving so many people frustrated and unfulfilled. What's my role in society? What's my true purpose? What's my life supposed to look and feel like? This book is timely and timeless, providing a proven system, with practical take-aways, that answers all of these critical questions. The world is craving authenticity, integrity, and connection, and Jimmy addresses these needs head-on, providing practical solutions for personal growth and societal change.

Let's be clear, this is not a quick fix—it's a lifelong commitment to being extraordinary, a pledge to be the most authentic version of yourself every single day. It's about honoring the responsibility you have, not just to yourself, but to those around you. Your growth, your transformation, will ripple out and impact others in ways you can't even imagine.

Don't just read this book; absorb it, live it, become it. Take action and watch how you transform, how your relationships deepen, and how your vision for the future expands. To everyone reading this— this book is what you've been waiting for. And as you turn each page, remember this: the world needs you. Not a version of you molded by society or tarnished with toxicity, but the authentic, powerful, and best version of you. Jimmy cares deeply about his mission and lives his life in a way that reflects that commitment. He can show you how you can do exactly the same thing in your life.

Don't hold back. Your journey begins now, and it's not just about you. It's about those around you, the community you live in, the family you love, and the legacy you will leave behind. Embrace this path of self-discovery and growth, for it will unlock doors you never even knew existed.

There's no time to waste, no reason to doubt yourself; the world needs good men, and you know it's time to be one, find one, or raise one.

Ed Mylett

Preface

"The only thing necessary for the triumph of evil is for good men to do nothing."

In December 2021, I founded We Are The They (WATT), a first-of-its-kind and rapidly growing coaching program. Through WATT, thousands of men and their families now have the resources, experiences, and network they need to become the best version of themselves. I directly mentor a wide array of members, from ex-pro athletes and established entrepreneurs, to everyday badasses and up-and-coming leaders. My long-time friend and previous mentor, Melissa, leads the Queens group, and the Next Gen group for teens is led by myself and many other outstanding men.

Before founding WATT, I had a 17+ year career in real estate, selling more than 2,500 homes, including the Utah real estate record for the most expensive private residence. My journey as a mentor began in that arena as well, coaching over 20,000 real estate agents and sharing my experience in two self-published books. But that's just "paid work." My life's work is to serve people and explore the world. I host *The Jimmy Rex Show* podcast (500 episodes and counting); I've traveled to over one hundred countries, and I've gone undercover to rescue children being trafficked with Operation Underground Railroad. Through those missions, I gained diplomatic status in Mexico and have memories and friendships that will last me a lifetime.

Building WATT is the most important thing I've done in my life. It's so transformational, it's hard for me to even know what to call it. Sometimes I say it's a "Coaching Group," a "brotherhood and a sisterhood," or other times I say it's a "movement." It's hard to describe because I've never seen anything like it. But at its core, WATT is a group of men, women, and teenagers committed to personal growth and supporting each other. Every member agrees to being authentic, vulnerable, and in integrity, three values you'll see interwoven throughout this book.

We Are The They might sound like a mouthful, but the naming origin is critical to what the group stands for. Several years ago, after returning from a dangerous undercover mission with Operation Underground Railroad, my girlfriend at the time said, "I really don't want you to do this anymore. It's super dangerous and a really bad environment." I responded, "Yes, but this is now part of my life's work. Did you not just hear about all the kids we rescued?" Her response was one of concern, "I know somebody has to do this but why can't they just do it?" Without thinking, I responded, "There is no they; we are the they!" Therefore, I wanted my own movement to attract members who aren't afraid to do something extraordinarily courageous—like taking ownership of their life and doing the work to be an unconditionally loving and holistically healthy human.

In today's world, the most challenging aspect for many men is finding a space where they can let down their guard, remove their facade, and be seen for their authentic self. Our society has constructed barriers that make it difficult to acknowledge our struggles, admit the problems we face, and voice the loneliness we feel. As a result, men don't have the tools to lead, wives are unsupported and overwhelmed, children aren't raised properly, and the foundations of our society are crumbling.

It's a troubling reality that it's so easy to use distractions to cope—be it work, sports, or more destructive escapes like alcohol, drugs, or pornography. These aren't simply vices; they are cries for understanding, a yearning for meaning, and quick ways to find a sense of self-worth. However, being ashamed for mistakes, actions that have caused harm, or poor decisions just perpetuates the toxicity that many people, just like me, must work to overcome.

After leaving the Church of Jesus Christ of Latter Day Saints, I began a 10-year journey of self-exploration. I did my best to revisit and reshape my beliefs about God, find my true life's purpose, heal family relationships, and learn about love. As a result, I found I was meant to be of service and as a result, created an extraordinary fulfilling life.

Friendships, community, and mentors made one thing clear: I couldn't go far alone. Throughout those years and still to this day, I seek out wisdom from esteemed coaches, mentors, and leaders. I read over 500 books in a decade and attended every possible event, mastermind, or retreat I was called to—my thirst for knowledge and growth was insatiable.

What was my key realization after so much learning? The love and validation I was seeking externally had been within me all along. Because of my childhood, I realized I tended to rely on others as well as unhealthy relationships to food, caffeine, and social interactions. After transforming my body, my mind, and finding peace within my soul, a burning question persisted: What next?

One day, my friend asked, "Jimmy, who comes to you for advice? What do they seek?" The answer had always been right in front of me. I realized just how many people reached out to me, expressing admiration for the life I led and a desire to learn how they could do the same. The men around me craved the same kind of close-knit friendships that I had.

That conversation marked the beginning of a new chapter in my life. I knew the best way to be of service was to create an environment that empowers people to change themselves, alongside brothers and sisters who are doing the same. That was my calling—to create a space for men, and now women and teens, to lead extraordinarily fulfilling lives. We Are The They is that calling come to life. Part coaching program, part community, but truly, at its heart, a movement that gives members the connection, purpose, and meaning, similar to organized religion, but without the dogma, hierarchy, or tendency for control. Many members are still active in their faith, but We Are The They is the day-to-day experience of what religions preach about.

The overwhelming response I received when launching this movement made it clear how needed it is. There is a clear yearning for community and a sense of belonging, but we are left unfulfilled by the short-term thrills of living a hyper-individualized lifestyle. We live in a time where material achievement is seemingly more important than meaningful experiences, loyal friendships, internal wealth, or holistic health.

This book is a guide to becoming and being exactly who you're meant to be, and a reminder of what it takes to live an authentically satisfying life. I'm grateful you are curious to do the work to be a healthy human even though we're living in such toxic times. I stand with you and am here for you, as we both become the goodness we wish to see, knowing there is no one else that will do it for us.

Acknowledgments

CREATING THIS BOOK has been an incredible experience. Looking back at my own journey, and the journey of the men of We Are The They (WATT) has been both therapeutic and energetic. Most people won't sign up for that path of introspection. A straightforward life is more than enough, they'll say. They don't need to understand why they do the things they do. They're not interested in letting others in through vulnerability. They'd rather go a mile wide and an inch deep. But I know firsthand you've gotta dig for the good stuff.

The men of WATT are different. Since day one they've played all out and embraced the path of self-awareness. I'm inspired daily by their courage and authenticity. Seeing a man put down his armor for the first time, in a room full of other men, and allowing himself to be seen is a beautiful thing.

This book is dedicated to them. Every single one of them. It's dedicated to those early believers who joined in December of 2021, not even knowing what they were signing up for. It's dedicated to those few, who saw the power of the first group and raised their hands to keep raising the bar. Thank you to every single one of you for trusting me with this process. Thank you for allowing me to be less than perfect, to learn as we grew together, and for rolling and adapting to my crazy ideas.

I'm so honored to help lead this group of humans, committed to becoming better fathers, husbands, sons, and friends. And it's not the big things, it's the many small moments of perfect connection that have validated all the other decisions I've made in my life. I used to wonder if I was on the right track, if my life mattered, if I was making the right choices. I don't worry anymore. The ripple effect of these perfect moments into the world have shown me, without a doubt, that it was all exactly as it was supposed to be. Every mistake I made needed to happen. Every decision I doubted was part of the process. While my life has been messy, it's been a beautiful mess. It all led to today where I get to witness the miracles and feel the love of this unbreakable brotherhood.

I love you guys. We're just getting started. We Are The They.

I'd also like to acknowledge Syris, who was the master at taking my words and putting them to paper. My best friend, Cameron, who saw the potential of this book and demanded it be everything it was supposed to be. To my coaches, Ed Mylett, Neil Strauss, Stefanos, Mel Abraham, Erwin Mcmanus, Melissa, and Kathy: it takes a village to keep me moving in the right direction. And to everyone else who has helped mold me and this program into what it needed to be. Thank you all. This book is a product of all of us and a testament to the power of your positive influence.

Introduction

"Waste no more time arguing what a good man should be. Be one."
—Marcus Aurelius

EVERY SINGLE THING you see around you was first created in somebody's mind before it became a reality in the physical world. Every great thing that's ever been made, like democratic governments, safe neighborhoods, or a healthy culture, doesn't happen by accident. They were created by great men and women that sacrificed and put in the effort to create it. Sadly, every evil and terrible idea that has surfaced in this world was also the creation in someone's mind before being made into a reality.

Misguided men are now trying to manufacture a world they want others with less resources to exist in. They are working hard to preserve their power and steadily gain more control of their fellow man. They have created it in their minds and are trying to force their will onto society. There's only one way to stop them. Good men and women have to create our own vision of the world and work harder than those who need us for their continued power.

That is how evil is eliminated, that is how we create a loving world, one which works for us and not against us. It's no longer okay to sit back and hope somebody else fixes the problems. Designs are being made for a world much less safe, much less accessible, free, and sovereign, and much less loving than the one we get to enjoy today. What will be your contribution? Where will you step in and help create a better world? What idea have you been sleeping on and been too afraid to create?

Many people talk about improving their lives, but very few bet on themselves and take action. Just by reading this book, you demonstrate your commitment to improving the quality of your life, your relationships, and the lives of those around you. No matter where you have been, what you have done, or who you have been, I promise, you will see a drastic improvement by investing your time, attention, and intention into these pages.

Waste No More Time

There has never been a more crucial point for those on this planet looking to make a difference. The economy is experiencing changes we've never endured before. Politics are more toxic than ever. Masculinity and morality are under attack from every angle. Men are being manipulated to mistrust their hearts and doubt their integrity. Womanhood is under attack, being reduced to derogatory names like chest-feeder, pregnant person, or extra-hole haver. While it is undeniably true that many men do exhibit toxic behaviors, I'm resolute that these contemporary trends miss on what true masculinity, femininity, and humanity are about.

We know that men have a special place in our society, raising strong children and honoring amazing women. However, many men are crippled with toxic behaviors that lead to significant trauma created within themselves, toward others, and their creations.

I have a confession. Starting my movement to help men level up in their lives and writing this book were the two scariest things I've ever done. I was terrified. It was confronting. I still often question myself on the best way to do things. And I'll let you in on a secret: people who write nonfiction books write about topics they've struggled to embody. That's why writing this book was a healing journey. It forced me to face every shadow, uncover every stone, and do my best to authentically and humbly share what I've learned in my process of becoming a man of integrity. But I did it. I answered the call because I know there are millions of men, women, and teenagers who need the tools, network, and resources to level up in life.

For me, the quote on the cover of this book and at the beginning of this Introduction perfectly encapsulates what we all must do. It's not only foundational; it's non-negotiable. We truly are living in toxic times. Can things get worse? Could we reach nuclear catastrophe? Could America enter into an economic "dark night of the soul" unlike ever experienced before? Without a doubt. But we don't have to! And even if we do, it's up to you, and every individual, to do the work to be that which we want to see in the world.

Therefore, we must "waste no more time." You must act now and do so daily. Like the name of my movement, We Are The They, there is no "they" coming to do what you alone can do. Secondly, there is SO MUCH NOISE in our modern world. So much arguing. So much division. Separation. Anger. Loneliness. Trauma. Abuse. Like I said, things aren't good, and they could get worse. However, by reading this book, you've joined a movement that's making things better. But you must also take action. In the depths of your soul, you know what you need to do. This book serves as a structure, guide, and reminder of what it means to be a good man.

So, waste no more time arguing or being distracted by others arguing about what a good man is or is not. It's time to BE ONE.

The Heart of This Book

Integrity is the quality of being honest, virtuous, and adhering to strong moral and ethical principles. It is the consistency between one's thoughts, words, and actions, reflecting your commitment to truth, fairness, and reliability. It's doing the right thing when it seems no one is looking. It's who you are behind closed doors and in the limelight.

Integrity is a fundamental aspect of personal development as it forms the foundation of your character. It influences your relationships, choices, and overall well-being. It builds self-trust, brings about positive interactions with others, and is the No. 1 characteristic to find and cultivate true fulfillment.

When Marcus Arelius said, "good man," he's speaking to the embodiment of integrity that only comes through taking informed, intentional action. While this book is predominantly written for men and young men, it's also written for those who love them, meaning single and married women, and mothers.

The chapter "Find One" is written for both men and women looking to get into a relationship with an authentically good man. I offer unspoken secrets, green flags, and red flags that everyone needs to know before, during, or after getting into a romantic relationship. The chapter "Raise One" is written for parents seeking to raise a man (or woman) of strong character. I also recommend that teens read this entire book.

You hold in your hands a blueprint that covers all areas of life, from mental health, friendship, creating a passionate work life, leadership, and so much more. This is the sole guide in being, finding, or raising a healthy man.

Notes for the Reader

At the beginning of each chapter, you'll find subtitles like, "From ASHAMED to LOVED," or "From IRRELEVANT to APPRECI-ATED." These are the transformations that you can expect to experience by reading and applying what's offered in that chapter. That being said, the ultimate transformation of this book is that you'll move from being FRUSTRATED to being FULFILLED. That's my promise to you.

My deepest intention is that by reading this book, you'll know exactly what you must do to overcome any toxicity within yourself, becoming a beacon of hope that it's possible to live an extraordinary and deeply fulfilling life.

I'm excited for you to dive in, and to fully embrace what you need to know to be a healthy man in spite of living in such toxic times.

As you dive into this book, I invite you to extend your experience with us at thebe1book.com/start. Here, in this specially curated online space, you'll find a wealth of resources that complement and enrich your reading experience.

1

Be Decisive

From ISOLATED to INSPIRED

"I learned that courage was not the absence of fear, but the triumph over it. The brave man is not he who does not feel afraid, but he who conquers that fear."

—Nelson Mandela

LIKE MILLIONS OF others, waking up early and getting out of bed used to be the hardest part of my day. To hold myself accountable and overcome this all-too-common weakness, I scheduled one of the members of my movement, We Are The They, to be at my front door waiting for me at 7:00 a.m. Every morning, I do a 45-minute walk, get to know them, and learn about what's going on in their lives. In this chapter, we're going to cover everything about mindset and why an accountability tactic like this is so powerful. I'm also going to tell you the most important story that I told one of my guys on one of these daily walks. When I think about mindset, I'm always reminded of hiking Mt. Kilimanjaro. I have a million lessons I learned on that mountain, but they can mostly be boiled down to two things: mindset and the people around you that impact your mindset.

The way I even came to do this hike is a story of its own. I was looking for adventure, so I called a buddy of mine, Jason Van Camp. This guy was a Special Forces commander and had over a thousand troops under his command. Needless to say, he's badass. I told him we should go do something crazy. Without missing a beat, he said, "Well, actually, if you ever want to climb Mt. Kilimanjaro, I'm in this group called the Waterboys. I think I could get you a spot." This group is something Chris Long (the second pick in the NFL Draft and 2× Super Bowl champion) started to build wells for families in Africa that don't have clean water. It wasn't long before Jason called me up and said, "Hey, Rashad Evans (Hall-of-Fame UFC fighter) just backed out. I think I can get you in! It's 10 NFL guys, 6 Special Forces guys, 1 Wounded Warrior, and then you, I guess . . . the realtor."

The day of the hike, I went with the six military guys; three Marines, two Green Berets, and a guy named Q, Phil Quintana. He was wounded in Iraq and would be climbing the entire mountain with one leg. I was shocked he was doing it, but deeply moved when I saw him. Q said he'd been training with one of the other climbers, a former NFL player named Dave Vobora. Dave was a middle linebacker for the Rams, an absolute giant of a man. After his playing days were over, he set up the Adaptive Training Foundation in Dallas, Texas. They take people from the military who have lost limbs and prepare them for things like climbing, ski jumping, or the like. Dave had been training Q for nine months just to climb this mountain.

In the morning, before we were about to leave, I had breakfast with Q. He was sitting by himself, and I wanted to get to know him. He was shy, but it didn't take long for him to open up to me saying, "The reason I trained so hard is because there are more men in my position than you realize, and we don't have much purpose or hope. It really sucks. So, I want to do this and show these other men what they're capable of."

Mt. Kilimanjaro is a six-day hike, with the first five days hiking over nine hours per day. It's intense, but also pretty basic—one step after another. But that sixth day is one you would never forget. Our second day out, I settled in next to Dave and told him how incredible it was that he'd trained Q to come out here. Knowing how hard the final push was, I couldn't help but ask, "Do you think he's gonna get to the top?" He looked at me and said, "Man, I sure hope so. Jimmy, I'm going to tell you a secret that nobody else knows. I've been training Q for nine months, but three months ago, I got a call in the middle of the night from his wife. He had a shotgun in his mouth, fully loaded, safety off, finger on the trigger."

Dave continued, "It's the third time within the last year that he's tried to kill himself, and we've had to talk him out of it. If this guy gets to the top of this mountain, he'll get over this barrier.

He'll find his own purpose, and he'll thrive. He's got two little girls at home. His wife is amazing. But if he doesn't get to the top, he'll be dead in six months." I thought we were just climbing a mountain. But after hearing that, I decided, "Okay, shit. Let's make sure *we all* get to the top of the mountain."

On day five, the last night, we got into the base camp about 3:00 p.m., ate, and tried to sleep for a few hours. Since it's so cold at the top, nobody could sleep so we were all just standing around trying to stay warm.

One of the military guys started asking everyone who we thought wouldn't get to the top. He turned to me and said, "I think it's going to be you." I wasn't offended; it was the predictable answer. Remember, I was just the realtor. The other guys were Marines, Special Forces, and professional athletes. The group leader heard this and was immediately irritated. "What are you talking about? We are all going to the top." The guy who singled me out figured this hike was all about physicality, but I knew better. It was all mental. I knew this mountain would be one of my life's hardest nights. But I made up my mind; I was going to the top. Not only for my own sake, but now that I knew Q's story, this hike was so much bigger than just me. I had made my decision.

Six hours into our last night, the guy who questioned my ability to finish was gone. I asked a few people what happened, and they said he wasn't feeling good, so he turned back. He ended up being the only person who didn't make it to the top that night. His very line of questioning showed his mindset. He had made it possible that someone might not reach the top. For him, it was an acceptable outcome to quit. His attempt to deflect his worries and fears on others was a mirror of what was really going on inside his own head and heart. So, I'm sure you're wondering, "If that guy quit, what happened to Q?"

If you've ever climbed Mt. Kilimanjaro, you know you have to keep the false summit in mind. The false summit is about six hundred feet below the real summit. It's the hardest part because it's so hard to breathe. I couldn't even think straight. It was, and still is, the most brutal thing I've ever experienced. And yet, Q was crawling on his hands, all cut up, heading for the top. We were supposed to be at the summit at 7:00 a.m., but we were way behind because Q was struggling. I watched him fall 50 different times and really mess himself up. It wasn't pretty, but he was determined; he was inspired.

I happened to be at the front near the two leaders of the groups, and I overheard them saying, "He's done. He's given everything. Let's get him down. It's getting dangerous." Hearing that, all I could think about was what Dave had told me. I was just the realtor; I had no say, but I knew Q couldn't stop. I panicked, thinking, "Shit, no, no, we can't do this." I frantically looked around, and finally, I saw Dave.

I ran over to him and said, "Dave, they're trying to get Q to go down. You've got to do something!" He stormed over and grabbed Q saying, "Listen here! You're not done yet. You're going to the top! If we have to carry your ass, we're taking you to the top!" All Q could do was nod "okay." Then, Dave turned to the group leaders and said, "This guy is going to the fu*king top!" We threw his arms around us and began to help him make the final climb. This was a great idea . . . for about 40 seconds. We all took turns and helped him get to the top, but he was done. It took Dave and I and several others to be there for him when he had nothing left on the descent. It took all of us to help him get across the finish line.

This story always makes me emotional because it was truly a life-or-death thing. There was no way Dave was going to let Q not get to the top. When Q was finally helped to the summit, Dave was there and kissed him on his forehead. I knew what that kiss meant, and it was the most beautiful thing I'd ever seen.

To succeed in life, only you can make that decision. It has to be a conviction that you will give everything you've got, no matter what. This could be being a more present father, successful in business, more accepting of your family, or standing up against toxicity in your friend group, community, and our society. But you don't have to do it alone.

Find somebody in your life who will be your Dave Vobora, someone who won't let you quit even when everyone else says you're done, and you start to believe them. Find that person; find the mentor, the coach, or the friend that you can count on when you're spent, and you have nothing left. Someone to help you keep going when you've given more than anybody expected, but you're not quite to the top.

The 5 Pillars of Success

Q's success did not happen by accident. There were 5 critical pillars that carried him through. These 5 pillars will show up throughout the book and they are the foundation for succeeding in every stage of your life.

While I don't claim to have it all figured out, what I do know is that when you're as committed to growing as I am, it takes constantly fine-tuning each one of these pillars.

1. **Make a decision and take a moral stand.**
   - This is a serious decision and is something you make between you and God. I'm not talking about something you decide to do on a whim or because you feel like it. This is a sacred pact, an oath, a pledge, a single choice that will dictate your entire life. It's how you take hold of your destiny and choose to live an extraordinary life.

     Like Q, falling hundreds of times, will you keep deciding to do what is right? How badly do you want it?

     Don't waste time arguing what good morals are or aren't. You know. You know exactly what the things are that you need to do. If you want to be successful, you have to make powerful decisions and stand for what you believe.

2. **Change your behaviors.**
   - Ultimately, living with better behaviors is what this book is all about. In Chapter 2 we will cover claiming your story free of shame, finding love for yourself, and the importance of building an inspired mindset. Do just these three things and you will live a successful life.

     But this is just the beginning of the rest of your life. Without committed action, your word means nothing. When things fail, fall short, or don't happen as expected, it's up to you to reevaluate your behaviors.

3. **The secret sauce is proximity—upleveling your friend group.**
   - By reading this book and doing the work, you'll start to find the right people and begin taking care of the relationships you already have.

     My friendships, relationships, and network are some of the things I'm most proud of, and while we've all heard it a million times, you really do become the people you spend the most time with.

     Don't use people and be opportunistic, but instead, come into new or old relationships with a servant-heart. Do this, and doors will open like never before.

4. **Be consistent and accountable.**
   - Unleveling your friend group will help you with this pillar more than anything, but it's still your choice to stay committed. Most people who want to succeed do everything up to this point, but when they see what it really takes, they turn back.

     Don't even give yourself the option. Don't be like the Marine who asked, "Which one of you isn't going to make it?" Instead, keep putting one foot in front of the other, knowing that doing the work to summit the mountain will put you in a position to be there for others when they need it.

The point of being successful isn't just about conquering the mountain, but who you do it with, and who you can help do the same.

5. **Invest in mentoring.**
   ■ Every good story has a villain *and* a mentor; both are essential for the main character's journey. Without a villain, we don't ever learn about the hero's true character. Without a mentor, they're living with limited perspective.

   Good mentors will transform your life for the better. Also, the fact you have this book in your hands is a result of me investing into a mentor who connected me with my publisher, getting this book released in record time.

   I wouldn't know what true success is had I done it all on my own. The phrase, "It's lonely at the top," is true, but not in the way most people think. It's not lonely when you have a mentor that shows you the way and other people you take the journey with. As shown by Q, he wouldn't have ever made it to the top without Dave being there as his mentor.

Being Decisive = Being Extraordinary

Things change when we make a committed decision—the universe begins to conspire in our favor. When we make a serious decision, things will start happening for us that couldn't have happened otherwise. It's like God is waiting to give us what we want. But until we make that decision, nothing's going to really change.

Most people wander through life, and they don't really know what they want. They don't think about the decisions required to get the life they want. They don't take control, they just let things happen to them. They become friends with people they live by; they take the career that falls in their lap; they end up getting married to the first person who is nice enough to them, and so on.

Trust me, that's not the way to become extraordinary. That's not the type of life that will test you, so you learn your true character. If you're not tested and don't know who you really are, when the going gets tough, who's to say what kind of person you'll be? Will you respond to a toxic situation with more toxicity? Will you be the hero or the villain in your own story?

By remaining indecisive long enough, people naturally begin to wonder why they feel so unfulfilled. Passive people will go to remarkable lengths to stay that way. Extraordinary people have the courage to create their life by design. To live a meaningful and successful life, you must make and stand by that decision.

To decide means to "cut off." When you finally decide what you need, you must cut off what no longer serves you and chart a course to a new life. The kind of decisiveness I'm talking about here is revolutionary. It's passionate. It's serious. There's a huge consequence if you fail. It's that one moment that changes the entire course of your life. It's not just, "I'm going to get off alcohol." It's, "I'm doing this, come hell or high water. I am going to make this happen because my life is going to be better because of this decision."

No matter what you want to do, there will be trials and tribulations and setbacks along the way. You need that level of conviction to stay the course. If you haven't truly decided, if you haven't made up your mind of what your life is going to be, when that trial comes, you will take the easier path. Unfortunately, that's what happens for most people, and they end up in this very average or below average life.

The word *average* means the median. That means most people are going to be average. But the key is to ask yourself two questions. First is, "How do I become my highest and best form of myself?" Second is, "How can I help raise the average of everyone around me?"

While there is nothing "wrong" with living a below average life and you could spend a lifetime self-justifying why being average is a good thing, why do so when you were born to be extraordinary?

Tony Robbins often says, "Decisions *not* conditions, determine our destiny." If you really believe that, you'll place yourself in unique positions to have unique experiences and live a unique life.

I decided to hike Mt. Kilimanjaro. Dave decided to tell me the stakes of Q making it to the top. I decided to tell Dave when the others wanted to send Q down. Dave decided to get in Q's face and let him know there was only one place he was headed—to the top. Then, we all took turns helping him climb from the false summit to the top. And from the first day to the last step, Q decided to keep going, bloody, crawling, and getting up time and time again until we helped him into a new mindset about himself, his life, and his purpose.

We all decided, and because we did, we're here to tell this story.

You know who else made a decision? That Marine who decided to quit. He let doubt creep in. When he said, "I think it's gonna be Jimmy that doesn't go to the top," my exact response to him was, "They will have to drag my dead ass off this mountain because I ain't coming back till I go to the top." That was my decision.

He had decided to do the hike when it was convenient. When you're sitting on your couch, and it's warm and your feet don't hurt, you can make a lot of decisions. I can tell people I want to get in the ice bath every single morning. But when it's two minutes in, and I can't feel my freaking guts, I have to decide if I'm really committed to the ice bath or not.

It's easy to just say that I'm going to be celibate for three months. But after a woman sends me a leading text and says, "Hey, what are you doing? I'm visiting my sister down the street," did I really decide or not.

Don't become someone who makes decisions only when it's convenient. For instance, when I was in real estate school, I committed to becoming one of the top agents in the state, reaching in 2 years where most agents get to in 20. Every subsequent action I made with that ultimate decision. I invested heavily in marketing and coaching, worked relentlessly, took extraordinary actions, and ultimately, achieved my goal. If you haven't made the decision of where you're going, then you'll end up falling to the temptations of an easier path.

Now that I've consistently lived by the 5 Pillars of Success, people often come up to me saying, "I want your life. I want to do what you do." Depending on the person, I'll respond with something like, "You can't just have my life. I built this. I did this on purpose. You can't just have what I have because you're probably not willing to do what I did. Instead, do what you need to do to have your own life that is by your own design."

People want the result without the work, but the problem is that you can't appreciate it unless it's really your own. I could have taken a helicopter to the top of Mt. Kilimanjaro, but I wouldn't have felt accomplished. The product of being clear with your decisions is that you end up with the life that's yours and one that you want. Only then can you become self-amused at the beauty and ridiculousness of your own life.

Who's Going to Be Your Dave Vobora?

Who are you able to go to war with? Who are the people supporting you? Who is your accountability, your community, who will support you no matter what? In the process of becoming extraordinary, you're going to get to a point where you're done. At some point or another, we all mentally break down. Even the people who care the most about you and want the best for you, sometimes they'll think you're done. That's when you need a mentor, the 5th pillar of success.

Often, people don't know how important things are to us. They don't always know why we have to do or believe certain things, and that's okay. But we need to have a mentor, so in those moments when we're done and ready to quit on our commitments, they won't quit on us.

Doing something that requires you to trust other people is what self-awareness and mindset are really about. Once you've decided what you are going to do, there's nothing more beneficial than doing it with other people. Q did everything he could. He gave everything, but he was done. We were three hours behind, the man fell 50 times, he was crawling, but he was done. In his own words, he "had nothing left in the tank." He gave everything just to get to that false summit. That's the whole point of having people with you. You're going to hit a place where you've got nothing left in the tank. That's where a mentor or a community picks you up.

You're Never Alone

You can't be fulfilled, let alone make a difference in the world by being isolated. People who are isolated are more prone to sickness, mental illness, physical disease, and sadly, suicide. The statistics of suicide aren't pretty, especially for men. And with the ever-growing use of social media, now, more than ever, we're losing thousands of teenagers. Loneliness is an epidemic.

People have lost connection to themselves and each other. If someone says they're a part of a community, we're more likely to imagine a Facebook group than an actual in-person gathering of people with a common purpose. We're more isolated than ever before, across every demographic.

One of our core human needs is human connection, sharing our feelings with people who care, and having a community. That's why I started We Are The They and why I consider it a movement. It gives members a place to explore and discover what it means to be a good man. This is changing their lives, their families' lives, and everyone who knows them. If *their* world is changing, then *the* world is changing. We don't waste time arguing what a good man should be but give each other the tools, resources, and network we need to BE ONE.

The stats make it clear that almost *all* men, even those who have been in the community for months, struggle with loneliness, depression, and suicidal impulses. But the beauty of the movement is that it gives members a safe place—a loving, diverse, and compassionate community—to share their experiences with. Instead of staying isolated, they begin to live inspired lives. This transformation is frequent, but the path to get there can be scary.

During a breathwork session at one of our events, a member and close friend of mine was able to tap into something he never knew was possible. Five years earlier, he had gotten his girlfriend pregnant, convinced her to have an abortion, and gaslit her to think it was her fault. They ended up staying together and had three more children. But after all those years, he carried deep guilt and shame that he convinced his girlfriend, now wife, to get rid of the baby.

In that breathwork session, he was able to talk to his child, and they told him, "Dad, it's okay. I'm in a beautiful place, and I love you. You did what you thought you had to do." Instantly, he had deep relief around something that caused him so much pain. Since shame festers in the dark, he'd never been able to share this with anyone. When he first got up, the first thing he said was that he had a gun to his head the night before. He had been suicidal for those five years, fighting this shame, but in that moment, he was able to let it go. You never know when or how long somebody has been suicidal.

His whole life he thought that if anybody knew this, they'd know how horrible of a person he was. But in that room, he got as vulnerable as he'd ever been and shared what happened. A grown man, bawling his eyes out, overcame his isolation and immediately, the entire room engulfed him in love, hugged him, and was simply just there with him.

The magic of being vulnerable is that it invites vulnerability in others. Soon after, another guy shared how he also forced an abortion and never talked about it. It didn't take long before everyone in the room shared their own reasons for isolation. These were strong, vulnerable men having breakthroughs of a lifetime, sharing tears and connection with their newfound brothers. This setting was possible because of the community we all created. Without it, they would have stayed feeling separate, not knowing what to do other than try and survive another day. But in that moment, so many men finally realized that they were lovable, despite the horrible things they thought defined them.

If someone keeps themself isolated, they're never going to be able to look at their life and smile at it. They're going to make the decision to remove and protect themselves. They're unlikely to do the hard things that will make their lives immeasurably better.

That's why suicide is the most intense decision ever because it is the ultimate act of control. It's the most immediately consequential choice anyone can make, and it's also the most ego-driven. All the other options slip away as the tunnel vision of feeling terrible, the identity of "being terrible," takes over our thinking and keeps us isolated. If you make one decision to live your life in a more vulnerable, authentic, and integral way, and really commit to it, it's going to change your life for the better. It may take longer and require more effort, but it's going to remove the need for that ultimate, and tragic, decision.

Remember, to decide is to cut off. So instead of cutting off the ability for people to love you, decide to do something truly inspired. It's the simplest of things that are the most extraordinary.

Be the Hero of Your Story

Even though I've not personally struggled with suicide, I've coached many men who have, including my best friend. As I was mapping out this book, I leaned on him heavily for insight. I'll share his full story in Chapter 7, and how my hunch to fly and see him changed both our lives. For now, I hope what he shares in the following might help you or someone you know who struggles with suicidal thoughts or behaviors.

Once you start to think about it as a real option, it makes you feel like you're trapped, like there's nowhere to go. The things that normally bring you joy or feel good just don't do it anymore. It's like you're never gonna feel like you once felt, so it's really hard to get back to a baseline.

Then, when loneliness sets in, it seems like there's no use talking to anyone because they're not going to be able to help. No one can help you, no one can understand you, and no one can do anything about it. If you reach out, then you're going to be a burden to people; you will just bring them down. Eventually, it feels like your existence is like a burden on yourself.

Then, once you feel like everybody would be better off without you there, that's the darkest point. But within that, you get to this place where it actually starts to make some sense that you're just freeing yourself and others from this pain. Everyone else might be sad for a little bit, but they'll be better off anyway. They'll forget.

While there's this hopelessness, there's also a primal desperation to change it. But the worst part is feeling this desperation but having a lack of motivation to do anything. This is why the only way out is by being honest with yourself and vulnerable with someone else.

But talking about it with someone can, and often, makes it way worse. Some people are very uncomfortable and they're afraid of talking about suicide, or even just anxiety, depression, or feelings in general. When you're in these dark places, you can easily sense somebody who's afraid of what you're experiencing.

A lot of times, I've found that when I bring someone into what that experience is, they'll energetically pull away or start to manage me. I now know it comes from a place of them wanting to help, but really, they're making sure that they're not responsible for pushing me over the edge.

But once I found safe places and people, the most helpful thing was being able to be completely honest with somebody about what I was experiencing. And then, just having them accept it and accept me, they joined me exactly where I was.

They didn't hurry the process, try to change my mindset, influence me, give me advice, dismiss it, or tell me to "look on the positive side." What we all need is someone who is willing to say, "I hear you, and I'm with you. None of this changes how I feel about you. We'll get through this."

It helps when someone else has been there too because they can echo some of the same feelings. The key is when telling someone what is going on, that there's no judgment, no fear, and to truly know that they accept you no matter what, exactly as you are. That will give you the permission to breathe and a hope to keep on breathing.

I still have this voice that appears every now and again. It's that negative voice that says things like, "You're not healed. You're not going to be okay. You're never going to get away from this." To be honest, I don't know how long it will stay. Thankfully, now that I've gotten used to reaching out, the bouts with them are less intense, and they're more spread out.

You have to learn to not pay too much attention to them, but at the same time, recognize the part of yourself that wants to die. The trick with suicide is that it's actually the part of you that feels hopeless, worthless, or unlovable that wants to die and be reborn into something new. If you can let those thoughts pass while also speaking your truth, you'll find deep healing.

That's why you need to have the right guys, mentors, and relationships around you to support you. You may need daily or weekly support because, for most of us, it's an ongoing thing.

What's crazy is that when we're in really dark places, we don't realize it, but the people around us often see us more clearly than we can see ourselves. Other people can help reframe the story we tell ourselves. To myself, I was imploding my family, my life, and my friendships. And it took Jimmy telling me, "You're the hero in this story." At the time, all I could see was that I was the villain. All I could see was the weak person who couldn't manage his own life.

But Jimmy saw someone who was enduring hardship and really fighting for something beautiful. Having other people in your life who will voice how they see you is invaluable. My isolation ended and my inspiration began when I started thinking, "Maybe I don't have the full story here. Maybe I'm not as bad as I think."

Be Decisive

Remember at the beginning of this chapter how I told you that I used to hate getting up early and used that powerful accountability tactic to overcome it? Accountability and isolation cannot coexist. Studies show, other than plant medicine, the best way to overcome addiction is through accountability. When we realize and find people that really care about us, we stop feeling isolated and start actually living.

When you live with integrity, everything in your life will be on point. Along with the other two Core Values of authenticity and vulnerability, they are the foundation of the 5 Pillars of Success.

As you increase in character and create a better mindset, you might get tripped up by something called "imposter syndrome." Imposter syndrome is when you feel like you don't deserve the success or accomplishments you've achieved and worry that others will find out you're a fraud. It's constantly doubting yourself and thinking you're not as good as you actually are. Even though you have evidence of your value, virtues, and success, you might still believe it's all just luck or that you'll be exposed as not good enough. This is an act of isolating yourself from your new truth. Don't fall for it!

To be an attractive, magnetic man, you have to recognize and redirect the whispers of imposter syndrome. Like my friend said, "You have to learn to not pay too much attention to them, but at the same time, recognize the part of yourself that wants to die." Tough love and being hard on yourself can be used for fuel, but it shouldn't be turned into a self-destructive fire.

To help my guys overcome imposter syndrome, I have them write down all the reasons why they are badasses. And I want you to do the same, right now. Go back to childhood all the way up to this moment—look for all the times you did something remarkable, broke records, and did things that you are proud of or were hard to do.

This list is yours. It could be filled with something that seems average, but it matters to you that you did it or completed it. You're making this list for yourself. It's a place you want to be honest, vulnerable, and also unashamed about! You've been through and accomplished a lot! So, write it down. Get 50 or more things you have experienced and accomplished that matter to you.

If you feel any hesitation making this list, don't get stuck by fear that's masquerading as humility. This is *your* list filled with things that matter to you and you alone. If you do this, and really fu*king go for it, you're going to see yourself with a new mind and become self-amused by the beauty and ridiculousness of your own life. And that, my friend, that is what it feels like to live life inspired.

You deserve that; everyone deserves that.

The next part of this exercise is just as important as the list itself. I want you to read the list any time you start to feel like an imposter, only you aren't going to read it as if you are reading it about yourself. Read it as if you are reading it about someone else, someone you've never met. You will quickly realize, "This person is amazing! I want to meet and be friends with this person."

For whatever reason, we are so quick to be impressed by others. We're so quick to give others credit for the accomplishments they have made, yet so slow to honor ourselves and see just how impressive we are. This small shift in how you view your own life will help you see what all your friends see—you are a badass.

So, waste no more time second-guessing whether or not you're a good man. BE ONE.

2

Be Shameless

From ASHAMED to LOVED

"If we share our story with someone who responds with empathy and understanding, shame can't survive."

—Brené Brown

BETWEEN THE AGES of 14 and 31, a good portion of my day was either thinking about baseball or sex. In most cases that wouldn't make me exceptional. Trying to hit triples in America's game and working just as hard to get to third base in the other activity isn't out of the ordinary for young men. My problem? I wasn't being guided by natural desire, and I was trying to outrun shame.

To understand shame, you have to first look at your environment. I had the double whammy of a restrictive religious upbringing and household where I didn't feel safe enough to be vulnerable. If I broke a church "rule" (and there were a lot) I knew I couldn't talk to my parents. Confessing to them would mean a loss of love, judgment, and a punishment to top it off. That meant my only other outlet was the church itself. I wouldn't escape judgment, but at least they couldn't ground me.

There were a lot of "don'ts" I had to contend with growing up. Don't have sex until you're married. Don't masturbate. Don't think about masturbating. Come to think of it, don't do anything even remotely sexual before you're married or the weight of the sin will crush you, and then, you'll be flat and won't be able to have sex anyway. Just don't. Most boys are scared about their first kiss; I was more scared about what God would think of me after it happened. How would I be judged?

When fear of judgment and loss of love creeps in, shame isn't far behind. My fear of not getting it right with God was so intense that I thought I was going to be struck down the first time I even touched a girl. Once, I was so ashamed about what I'd done, that I called my bishop at 1:30 a.m. in the morning. I couldn't bear the "sin" hovering over me and didn't want to die in a car wreck before I had a chance to fix it. And we're not talking about some crazy escapade, I didn't even have sex! That's the kind of thinking shame creates. Everything in my life relating to sex was riddled with fear and shame. No beauty or love in any of it. From high school to early college any memory of a sexual experience was coupled with a horrible feeling of shame.

When some people hear this, they don't really believe how much shame I had for acting on natural feelings of sexuality. But that's the thing about shame, it's an unhealthy mindset that turns healthy things toxic. And one of the first steps on the path to being a healthy man is shedding the shame mindset and moving toward self-love. You won't be able to love others until you learn to love yourself (mistakes and all).

I held onto my shame for years. It drove me on unhealthy paths to "success" and leaked toxicity into every part of my world: business, family, and romantic relationships. It took me over 30 years to figure out how to release it and I'll spend a lifetime helping others to let it go. So, listen up: to be a healthy man, you can't be stuck in the past or have any shame. You just can't. When it comes up, you have to explore it, resolve it, and release it. I'll show you how.

In this chapter, I'll lay out what shame is, the environments it thrives in, and how it can manifest in unexpected places. I'm going to be vulnerable about the wreckage and healing I encountered on my path to self-love in hopes that you'll find the courage to be vulnerable too. Finally, I'll show you how to do the work to release your shame like I did. Buckle up, this might be a rough one.

What Is Shame?

Guilt is: "I've done something bad." *Shame* is: "I am bad." Guilt *can* serve a critical personal and social purpose. It's important to recognize when you've done something that isn't in your best interest, or the best interest of others. Those realizations can drive positive change. The issues arise when we don't tackle *the action* of doing something wrong, but instead, we identify as *being wrong*. It seems like a subtle shift at first, but it's an incredibly dangerous change. How does this shift in mindset happen?

The world-leading expert on shame, Brené Brown, says the shame mindset thrives under three core conditions: secrecy, silence, and judgment. I felt like my sexual feelings had to be kept a secret. I'd only tell someone if I had to and even then, it was a struggle. For you, it might look like getting laid off from your job and not telling your family. You're in recovery, but don't want anyone to know. You look at internet porn but would deny it if asked point blank. Shame feeds on secrets.

I silently suffered for years about who I wanted to be on the inside and who I had to be on the outside. You think if you just hide in the corner with your drinking problem the drum beat of shame will fade away. But it doesn't. The bass kicks in, the symbols crash, and you're the only one that can hear it. Shame grows louder when you get quiet about your struggles.

And finally, there's the almighty judge: our crippling inner critic. There was clearly outward judgment of my actions by my church and community, but the worst character attacks came from myself. "Why did I do that?" "I'm awful." "I need to look leaner." "People will always remember this moment." Ever said any of those things to yourself? Shame invites judgment.

Once the shame mindset is established, you stop consciously being aware of your shame. When someone says something negative about you, or you've found yourself in an embarrassing or intense situation, the shame you feel invokes a trauma response. Some people will fight, some will look to avoid, while others will freeze up. Or if you've built up so much armor that keeps you numb, you won't even realize, "Oh, I'm feeling ashamed right now."

Shame is tricky because it feels like self-awareness. Just like you can be self-aware in a positive way as "I can, and want, to be better in this area," shame is the negative part that keeps you stuck in behaviors and beliefs that don't actually help you. You reaffirm an identity that isn't even true and block any path to change. Sure, there may be some truth to it, but what we all need is a chance to see ourselves as more than the lie of, "I am bad." What we need is a chance to see ourselves as worthy—someone who lives motivated by self-love, compassion, and forgiveness, not judgment and shame.

I was raised to believe if I did anything the church said was wrong, I should feel ashamed. That didn't help me do and be better, it only left me feeling unlovable and alone. Eventually I found a way out. And you will too. But first you have to speak your secrets and break the silence.

The One

I lost my virginity when I was 31. That's right, a 30-year-old virgin. Keep in mind, I was raised to believe that my sole objective in life was to serve the church and find *the* one. And finding *the* one meant saving yourself for *the* one. I held out as long as I could on the saving myself part, but I never gave up on the searching. This was the mission of my life and finding *the* one consumed me, sunrise to sunset. I'd already established my business reputation in door-to-door meat sales and then real estate, and I was making good money. But financial success was always secondary or a means to an end. What mattered more than anything else was getting married (or so I thought).

After a few years, and literally going on over a thousand dates, I thought my search was over. I was in love. Even her month-long trip to Thailand soon after we started dating couldn't stop me. I would wake up at 6 a.m. to FaceTime with her every day. I stopped dating other women and could feel the weight of finding *the* one being lifted. I was fully in. However, I must add, it was a complicated time as I worked through a crisis of faith and was open to women outside of my church for the first time, but I was convinced I'd found the girl for me.

One morning, right before our daily FaceTime, I woke up thinking about how to win this girl over and ways to make her life better. I'd worked out all the angles with my life coach and just needed to put my plan into action. Unfortunately, she wasn't in on the plan. After a bit of small talk, she casually said, "Just so you know, I don't like you the way you think, and I don't look at you as *the* one for me. I just like talking to you." I was crushed. Absolutely devastated.

Already scrambling to figure out what my new moral compass was outside of the church, I didn't know what to do. I was hurt and angry and wanted the pain to go away. I went out partying that weekend and had sex with two different girls. Immediately, the inner voice started to rumble. "This isn't like you." "You shouldn't have allowed yourself to do that." The hot waves of guilt and the internal shame shit storm washed over me: "I am so bad. I'm not good enough. I'm never going to be fulfilled."

You're Not Good Enough

I didn't always think I was bad or not enough. Little kids don't throw a ball and think, "I'm bad at this." They think, "Look what I did!" It's when other people add their two cents, and you start to believe it, that things go south.

When I was 14 years old, I was faced with a difficult decision. I wasn't very good at baseball, yet baseball was my life. I'd just been cut from the all-star team and only six or seven players my age would make the high school team. My dad proposed holding me back a year to help me grow, get stronger, and become a star on the high school baseball team. A few kids at a nearby school had done it and they became state MVPs. While I now believe he had my best interest in mind at the time, this was *not* okay with me. I loved my friends, I was already one of the oldest kids in my grade and was one of the smartest kids. I did not want to get held back.

We went back and forth until the decision had to be made. "You need to decide now. Are you going to get held back?" I told him no. The next part of the story is tough for some to understand, but again, baseball was my life. He looked me in the eyes and said, "Just so you know, if you don't, you're not good enough to play high school ball, and you'll never play again." What do you think is the only thing I heard? "You're not good enough."

I decided to use his judgment as my motivation. "I'll show him!" And I did. That same day, I wrote "You're Not Good Enough" underneath my orange and black hat. For the next three years, that stared at me in the face every time I took the baseball field. His words lit a fire under me that burned just below the surface. Not only did I make the team, but I was a starter, and one of the top hitters on the team my senior year. Memories of a lifetime. His words had worked, but it would be another 17 years to understand what they'd really done to me.

How to Get Rid of Shame

The only way to get rid of shame is vulnerability. It's that simple. Simple, but not easy. I'll show you how simple it is and just how hard it was to get there. Let's get back to my long-distance heartbreak and subsequent "two-night stand." My shame spiral was cut short as I had a scheduled call with my life coach, Melissa (who is now my business partner in my coaching program). Keep in mind that our previous call was coming up with fun things *the* one could do in Thailand. This call would not be the expected follow-up.

Instead of telling Melissa how well it was going with *the* one, I had to tell her I got my heart broken and then hooked up with two random girls. I already knew what was coming; I was a terrible person, and she'd confirm that for me. She'd play the role of the church leader and say some version of, "God will not be mocked." I was expecting (and thought I deserved) to be made to feel small, afraid, and ashamed. But what she actually said changed my life. Melissa, bless her, said, "Oh, my gosh, I'm so sorry, Jimmy. I wish I could hug you. You must be so heartbroken." Um, what? "Wait, you're not mad that I was with these girls?" I was floored.

She continued calmly, "I'm sure you were just doing whatever you could to try to feel good. But let's ask a couple questions. Did those girls get what they wanted out of it? Yes? Okay, were you smart about it? Were you safe? Yes? Okay. Jimmy, you didn't do anything wrong. Obviously, it's not the perfect situation, and I don't think you'd do it again. But it's very understandable for the circumstance that you're in."

This was the first time in my life where I didn't feel wronged for what I had done, especially regarding something sexual. I was completely confused. But even more, I was relieved. I'd finally stopped suffering in secrecy and silence, and I received the empathy that kind of courage to be vulnerable deserves. This conversation opened my eyes and propelled me to explore what life looks like liberated from shame.

I didn't have to tell Melissa what I did. I could have brushed off what the girl I thought I was in love with had said to me. I could have even canceled the call. I could have continued to hide and feed the shame loop. Instead, I took a chance with someone I trusted and was vulnerable. This completely changed my life, and it can change yours too.

Even if I had done something hurtful to one of those girls, like lied or led one of them on, the only way for me to heal was to be honest with myself and those I care about. I use this example because it was a powerful shift for me and lands on a positive note. But believe me when I say, I have done things to hurt people. In situations where we do cause hurt (especially in those instances), an even deeper level of vulnerability is required. Not only to heal and find forgiveness for yourself, but to approach those you've hurt and apologize with a humble heart. Be without shame but be careful of being shameless without humility. Pride only leads to more shameful actions, loneliness, and armoring ourselves from ever having to be vulnerable. Don't try to make yourself right, but do what your heart knows you must to live free from shame.

You're Most Lovable When . . .

Up to and including that powerful moment with Melissa, every sexual experience I'd ever had was riddled with shame and guilt. What I was doing with those I loved, no matter how casual or committed the relationship, was all driven by pain and a negative undertone.

Every intimate situation demands safety, consent, and utter respect. But being burdened by shame is toxic. If you're reading this book, I know you have a good heart and are living for more than just yourself. Because of that, the healthiest thing you can do is get vulnerable about what you feel you need to keep hidden. Releasing that secrecy will finally mean that when you're with someone, you can really be *with* them.

Melissa helped me accept myself and see that my heart was in the right place. Even though my coping mechanism wasn't the wisest option, she told me, "Jimmy, you're most lovable when you're vulnerable, authentic, and in integrity."

That's it. From the moment I heard those three words, they've guided my entire life. I was able to see, "Okay, while *my actions* were not good, that doesn't mean that *I* am not good." By feeling the emotions in that moment, I recognized that I was hurting, and I did something I thought would make me feel better. But that didn't mean I was bad. I realized, "Wow, she's right. I am a good person. I didn't do this because I'm a bad person. I know my heart." That realization of self-love instead of shame empowered me to make better decisions in the future.

It took me becoming vulnerable and authentic to not be ashamed of what I did. This increased my sense of integrity. Only then did I get out of the prison of loneliness and shame. When your life is guided by vulnerability, authenticity, and integrity, you're going to be a good, stable, and healthy man. These 3 Pillars are like a three-legged stool. You take out one, and you're unstable. But if you genuinely seek to add one or more back into your life, the stability and positivity in your life and relationships will be immediate. Let's dig in on how to release your shame and create a more honest platform for your life.

Releasing Shame Respectfully

All I can do is look back and smile at the mistakes I've made. I'm smiling because I know I've done everything I can to amend the impacts of what I've done in the process of becoming a man of integrity. That is doing the work of claiming my story free of shame with a humble, servant-heart. At first you might not get it right, I sure didn't as you'll see, but the act of releasing shame respectfully is critical to building a healing practice.

Remember when I called my bishop at 1:30 a.m. to confess that I had intimately touched someone I was seeing at the time? I was a successful, independent 25-year-old, but I had little-to-no emotional intelligence. Again, nothing to be ashamed of now, but the 25-year-old me could be quite an asshole. I felt so bad about being intimate with her, and not knowing what to do with that shame, I decided to dump it onto her. I shamed her for being the person that allowed me to do that. That's toxicity at its worst. I hurt her by making her the guilty party. But that didn't make me feel less shame, it multiplied it. My emotional armor got thicker, and inevitably, she felt used and taken advantage of. I felt so shameful that I had to cut her from my life even though in reality, neither of us did anything wrong.

I'm not proud of that story or the many other times I've hurt people to compensate for my own pain. But I am grateful to know that through those experiences, there is redemption for those who have an open heart. An important part of understanding shame is to explore and resolve the situations that have created it. Some things stick to us that would roll off someone else's back, so you have to be open-minded to whatever has hurt you and what you've done to hurt others.

Unfortunately, most people don't have the tools, community, or guidance to get free. But unresolved shame is the source of almost all toxicity. We're going to change that together. That's why this chapter is right at the beginning of this journey you're embarking on. When you can finally claim your own story, shameless *and* humble, you can begin to live a truly fulfilling life. It's time to step out of the shadows.

Shadow Work

We all have a shadow, which is the side of us that's disconnected and unrecognized by our true identity. It's the part of yourself that's been rejected since childhood. You likely have little awareness of it, but you know you're looking in the right place if you start to feel emotions like anger, fear, shame, or if you become defensive, belittle your feelings, or distract yourself.

Shadows are the facets of yourself that have been ignored or repressed, often due to the pain or embarrassment they stir up. These unseen parts are almost always associated with shame, blocking us from living our most authentic lives. So, if you want to live an extraordinary life and truly be a good man, you've gotta do the work.

Shadow Work is integrating the entire spectrum of your being. If you haven't come to terms with yourself or your entire personality, you will shift that baggage onto others and jeopardize healthy relationships. The key is finding self-awareness and self-love regarding your demons from the past, especially before they shift pain to your partner. Shadow Work demands an authentic vulnerability that many find daunting. Contemporary movements that are based on virtue-signaling and tearing down others just makes the shadows more elusive and obscure. Codependent or toxic relationships are the same—they allow us to project our own shadows onto another person and then blame them for all their flaws instead of pausing to recognize why we see those flaws in the first place.

What we need are environments where we can open up without fear of judgment or rejection. That's why Shadow Work isn't something we can do completely on our own. Most people unconsciously get into relationships attracted to what they need to heal instead of what's already been healed. We need relationships built on humility. We need communities founded on integrity, not ideology. We need movements that require self-sacrifice instead of condoning self-justification.

Only by shining light into our darkest corners can we begin to heal. By seeing our shadows, we remove the spell of shame that keeps us stuck living out the same patterns. By replacing your shameful parts with unconditional love, you will pull all of the pieces of yourself back together.

Those who shy away from their shadow cannot be trusted. They remain a danger to themselves and others. To be safe and trustworthy—aka a man of integrity—you must find the courage to be vulnerable. You must develop the conscience to be authentic. You must choose to be humble in the pursuit of doing good.

You're Good Enough

In December 2018, nearly 20 years after my dad told me that I "wasn't good enough," I finally faced that shame. I was doing a plant medicine journey and halfway through the night, my "motivational" hat flashed into view. With some life experience under my belt, and a clearer understanding of affirmations and the power of words, I realized what had been driving me. I wasn't motivated, I was propelled by the judgment of not being good enough.

Instantly, so many of my behaviors and personality made sense. Why did I always try to win everything? Shame. Why did I have to be the best at everything? Shame. Why was I obsessed with being the best missionary, the best realtor in Utah, have everyone see all the beautiful ladies I was dating, and create envy for the crazy experiences I was having? Shame.

What was really happening was my inner child screaming, "I promise I'm good enough! Look at what I just did!" And decades later, another voice came to that kid's rescue and said, "This has served you, but it no longer does. It's time to let it go." What a BEAUTIFUL message! It didn't say it never served me; it said it no longer did. Then, this voice said, "Your dad carries a lot of shame over this too. Go to him and help him find a release too."

That was the first night I ever experienced psychedelics, and I don't recommend calling your super religious dad in that state of mind. But I knew what I needed to do and say to him. I called and we had a beautiful talk. A huge wound was healed that day for both of us.

Tony Robbins often talks about the two biggest fears we have. These are:

1. We aren't lovable.
2. We aren't good enough.

We all have these fears. I just decided to pour gasoline on mine during the most pivotal time of my brain development by literally writing it where I could see it every time I did what I most loved. It served me in many ways and in many ways it didn't. I was relieved to let it go.

Since that day, I've had a new feeling of peace about just being me. I don't need to prove that I am lovable. I've been able to strive and accomplish things out of love and no longer from a place of shame. And you and I are exactly the same. You are fully capable, maybe more than you'll ever know. But every day we have to put in devoted effort to love ourselves and each other. Letting go of your shame or judgment-fueled motivations will not make you lose your edge. In fact, you'll sharpen your "why" with love and authenticity, and build a more fulfilling life than you could have imagined.

One of the first things I do for those who join *We Are The They* is tell them this story and give them a hat where I've written "You're Good Enough" underneath the bill. We need more men motivated by love, not shame.

I tell you all these stories to help you create a new vision of the future that's not defined by the past. To do this, you have to be okay with being seen and heard. Only then can you truly accept love from yourself and others. Only then will you be someone you're proud of, regardless of what's been done in the past. Imagine a world where this type of thinking was the standard. Imagine that world with you in it. Now go and make that world a reality.

3

Be a Warrior

From STUBBORN to STRONG

"You can either suffer the pain of discipline or the pain of regret."
—Jim Rohn

PHYSICAL HEALTH, DIET, exercise—I think we've all heard more than enough on this damn topic, right? So, you may want to turn the page and skip over this chapter. I get it. But I really hope you don't. Nowadays, we're overwhelmed with information about what is and isn't healthy, so what we need is simple and useful information. But if you look on store shelves, to social media gurus, and even legitimized scientific studies, it's all manipulated by corporate growth obligations and strategic marketing. What they're really after is your dollar; they don't give a shit about your health.

If you look at a picture of a beach in the 1950s or 1960s, everyone is fit, lean, and functionally healthy. Why? They were eating naturally grown foods, weren't taking medications, and lived active lives. But now, on top of our food sources being filled with toxicity from farm to table, dieting and physical fitness are highly contentious subjects. To make it simple, here are a few reasons why we're living in much more toxic times regarding our fitness and physical health:

- Processed, sugary, and fatty foods are the cheapest and most accessible. We've traded authenticity for convenience.
- We walk less, and many of us spend our time at work scrolling or streaming, not moving or physically working.
- The food and pharmaceutical industries systematically demonized things we've used for thousands of years. One example is replacing naturally occurring fats like butter, ghee, tallow, and lard with margarine, PAM non-stick spray, and other highly carcinogenic compounds.
- Mono-crop farming, herbicides, and genetically modified foods are causing diseases and cancers at rates never seen before.

Ultimately, there are too many cooks in the kitchen telling us what we should be doing and not enough of us actually growing, cooking, and eating nutritious food. But that's easier said than done—believe me, I know.

It's taken me years to get my daily diet and physical fitness dialed in. Out of all the chapters in this book, this topic is the one that makes me the most anxious to talk about because my health journey has caused me intense distress. At the beginning, other than playing sports, I only exercised because I wanted to be more ripped. It was based on selfish gain and for the attention of others. It was pure vanity. My initial ideas about diet were just as ignorant, but I came by it honestly. As a kid, I was raised at the baseball field, and every day after school, my friends and I were at the park. Before or after practice, at games, or just hanging out, all we had for dinner was the Snack Shack where I'd get a Snickers and hotdog, a chocolate donut, or my favorite Little Debbie snack. That's just what I lived off of; I didn't know any better. God bless my parents, but they didn't know the importance of good, healthy snacks. I literally lived off Swiss cake Rolls, Nutty Bars, and every other kind of processed food you can imagine. Inevitably, this lifestyle and food choices created an emotional attachment because those foods were what made me feel good. From a very young age, I became accustomed to eating bullshit. That's what became home for me. That's what made me comfortable.

When I first went to college, I thought I had upped my game and was eating "healthy": cereal, granola bars, macaroni and cheese, peanut butter and jelly sandwiches. By eating at home, I thought that made me healthy. Seriously, I really did. As you can see, I was about as ignorant as it gets.

Exercise and dieting properly never felt like it came naturally to me. I have to dig in and make it happen. In time, I've learned being strong, resilient, and capable feels much better than being comfortable. In this chapter, I'm going to cover health, wellness, and fitness in a commonsense way that's needed now more than ever. As driven men, we often neglect our health for other priorities. But physical health cannot be separated from our overall well-being. For you to become truly healthy, you have to make it a part of your identity, starting right now.

Being healthy, eating healthy, working out, and all of the things that come with it, can be life-changing values or just temporary changes. It's important to take what you learn here and make it part of who you are. Together we'll create a new vision of your current and future self.

What Is a Warrior?

A warrior is a person who shows great virtue, courage, and determination. The way I'm using the term here, a warrior is not someone who incites violence, but rather, knows how and why to do the absolutely essential work to be strong, capable, and powerful. True power is knowing what you're capable of and choosing peace. Being stubborn or being weak but justifying it as "normal" or that you "love yourself" is not strength. That will wreck your integrity because no matter what you tell yourself or society tells you, you'll know you're lying to yourself.

As the hero of your own story, you must not see villains or enemies as something separate from you. A hero is only a hero because he's tempted by the villain, knows he's no different, but chooses the more virtuous path. A hero who is never tested is harmless, and a weak warrior is not to be trusted.

Can and should everyone love themself exactly as who they are? Absolutely and unconditionally. But I don't work out because I hate my body. I work out because I love it, and so should you. Masquerading unhealthiness as "self-love" or other excuses will only lead to illness, not wellness. There's an agenda to normalize obesity, which is devastating to adults and especially children. Look no farther than what I just told you about my childhood. I was completely ignorant to what being healthy was. I didn't know any better. But later in life I was willingly ignorant. I'd play games and lie to myself, knowing that fast-food burgers, RockStar energy drinks, and donuts were anything but healthy. But then I decided. I decided to "cut off" that ignorant version of myself and move forward.

When I became vulnerable about my insecurities, and honest with myself about what needed to change, I took the first step toward getting into integrity with my body, mind, and soul. I was on the path of the warrior.

Technically, a warrior is someone who wages war, but truly, a warrior is someone who is capable of protecting the kingdom at all costs because he trains. Every day he takes up his sword, but never to harm. Every day he refines his craft, but never to prove himself. Every day he gets a little bit stronger and a little bit faster because he knows he'll need it when he's tested. He does this every single day because he knows, one day, a threat to his kingdom's well-being will come, and he must be prepared for an attack on his integrity. Instead of chasing after a fight or looking for a challenge, he keeps his sword sheathed, knowing exactly what he is capable of.

A warrior knows his true self because he trains every single day, making steady progress. A true warrior does not train from a place of fear or insecurity. Warriors who train from a position of devotion, growth, patience, and virtue are the ones who reap the rewards of the entire process.

We live in confusing and toxic times, yet you must not waste any time arguing about what is or is not healthy. Instead, simply put in the work to better yourself. Being extraordinary is your choice, and having physical strength is essential to be a healthy human. Instead of looking at other people as a measurement of who you are or what you need to do, you must create a vision of your own self. By doing this, you'll cultivate a confidence and strength that no one can take away. Knowing your power, you'll have no need to fight, argue, or waste time because you'll be busy being a good man.

And if this all sounds too serious, I'm going to ensure this journey is joyful. Nothing will change your confidence more in your life than loving how you see yourself in the mirror. This is not just an actual mirror and looking at your body, but looking at the mirror within yourself, reflecting on your true identity and finding love for who you are. You are in control of that inner version of yourself. Only you control what you eat, what supplements you take, and how willing you are to workout. Only you control what you see in the mirror.

Poison Here, Poison There, Poison Everywhere

Throughout my twenties and thirties, I put a huge emphasis on work, spiritual growth, money, and other areas because I thought I'd always been in decent shape. I was athletic; girls seemed to like me; I felt good enough; I never had physical injuries; I ran a marathon, and hell, I climbed Mt. Kilimanjaro. Since I was physically able to do everything I wanted, I didn't even realize I was justifying my unhealthy habits. I could push through and do super intense things, but my day-to-day lifestyle wasn't dialed. If there was something I wasn't physically able to do, I'd find a way to justify that too. That's how self-justification works; no matter the reality, there's always some circumstance or excuse that gets you off the hook.

I was choosing to focus on how I was "fine" rather than acknowledge what needed to change: my diet was still full of terrible foods, I drank too many sugary drinks, my caffeine intake was off the charts, and I was getting accustomed to alcohol after 30 years of being without it. Sure, I was good enough to do the things I wanted, but when I was shirtless in my bathroom, I knew I had work to do. That last sentence could be read as self-judgment and a "toxic masculine" trait, but it was an absolute fact that I could be doing much more to take better care of my body. It finally hit me that my complacent sense of self was exactly how people become average.

When I was at Tony Robbins's *Date With Destiny* event, he said something I didn't understand at the time but is crucial to my current mindset. **"When you have your health, you have a million other wants, but when you don't have your health, you just have one."** I'm grateful it didn't take a health scare, illness, or disease to wake me up to the absolute fact that I needed to shift into integrity with my diet and fitness.

It was easy to be unhealthy in my early years when I truly didn't know any better. My friends were in decent enough shape, most of my family was just a little overweight, and for most of the people in my world, it simply wasn't a priority. We really do become like the people we're around. It took time for me to digest that we are made up of what we take in. If you're taking in bullshit, your body is not going to be optimal. Eating food that was accessible and cheap didn't have many instant negative impacts, but it was the fuel my brain and body used to grow. And since my brain wasn't being supported with good nutrition, it was easy for my weak mind to jump into self-criticism. Bad things in; bad thoughts arise, and more bad decisions.

A common mistake is thinking physical health is simply a physical act. Then we can tell ourselves the lie that, "I'm just going to have more discipline." But that misses the root of the problem. There's an underlying reason beyond lack of willpower for why we overeat, use food for mental comfort, and try to make ourselves feel better. Food is a great way to escape difficult emotions. Like an addict, we return to the things we know are bad for us because it makes us feel good in the moment.

I desperately wanted to break my negative eating habits, but I couldn't stop eating bullshit. When I was working in real estate, the first part of my day was doing cold calls. To make myself feel better about facing this difficult task, I would "treat" myself to a blue Rockstar and a maple bar. Actually, I'd go to a certain gas station where I could get two for $3. I'd start my day with an injection of sugar and caffeine that made me feel amazing. That first hour on the phone, I was hyped. Then, halfway through, I'd take a break and down the second Rockstar. For years, I literally started my day with a donut and two energy drinks. Yikes!

By the time I was done with my calls, I'd feel a great sense of accomplishment. I started to correlate the blue Rockstar with getting something done, not the act of sitting down at the damn phone and getting to work. As is the case with all addiction, I got hooked on the ritual. I wasn't addicted to energy drinks; I was addicted to that specific blue Rockstar. The white Rockstar didn't do it for me, and any new flavor release left me disappointed. No Monsters, no Red Bull. None of them gave me that blue Rockstar "feeling." When I took the time to unpack this ritual, I was able to recognize the emotional attachment I'd placed on these "foods" (if you can even call them that). The maple bar donut was the exact same thing. There would be some days when I wasn't even working, I felt lethargic, and I wanted to feel accomplished. I'd go get a maple bar, and all of a sudden, I felt like my day was back on track.

At the height of this era, I went to a Tony Robbins event in Fiji. We did a four-day juice cleanse, and believe me, there were no blue Rockstars on that island. There wasn't even sugar or caffeine. I was unsettled to say the least. By Day 2, I felt awful. On Day 3, I was absolutely miserable. The guy leading my group asked us, "So, how's everybody feeling?" Everyone was like, "Oh, I feel great!" When they got to me, I told them the truth. "I feel awful. I feel as bad as I've ever felt in my life." The leader, who now happens to be a part of We Are The They said, "Oh? Can you tell us about that?" I shared that when I woke up, there was a gross gray film on my sheets. Clearly, I had some major toxins in me that were purging out.

By the fourth day, I felt clear and good. I'd forgotten what it felt like to feel healthy. I knew I was done with that daily ritual, and I was never going back. I made the decision to never drink another blue Rockstar in my life. I haven't had one in four years and counting.

I'd made a step in the right direction, but I still had to resolve the underlying emotional attachments to what I put into my body. If I hadn't, that blue Rockstar would have just turned into some other junk to feed my feelings. What happened next was brilliant. At that event, Tony spent over five hours teaching us about how we were poisoning ourselves. He gave us three ways to get healthy, which may seem simple, but it's not so simple to apply: Stop poisoning yourself, cleanse yourself of the shit that's in you, and then put good stuff in.

These conscious logical practices helped me override my previous unconscious decision-making. I agreed that I didn't want to poison myself. Therefore, the maple bars, blue Rockstars, fast food, sodas, alcohol, and many other things literally became a poison. The alcohol was harder to kick, but I did a water fast and I quit immediately after. During that four-day water fast, it hit me clearer than ever that our body is literally made up of whatever it is we're taking in. No wonder I was overweight when I ate a donut every day, it was literally what I was made of. If you're drinking alcohol all the time, you're literally poisoning your cells.

Cellular regeneration is the process where every cell in your body eventually remakes itself. Depending on the type of cell, it takes longer than others. If you commit to changing your lifestyle and you only give yourself healthy things, your body will no longer crave those poisons. If you completely quit eating sugary, processed, and cancerous foods, it takes about two years for your body to be fully cleansed of those things. Trust me, it's worth the momentary discomfort. Do this, and you might just get your life back.

Done Is Better than Perfect

I don't work out because I hate my body. I work out because I love it. It's out of self-love that I've hired a lot of coaches and people that are smarter than me to keep me accountable and up-level my lifestyle. This action alone encapsulates the entire 5 Pillars of Success: **Make a decision and take a moral stand, change your behaviors, level-up your friend group, be consistent and accountable, and invest in mentoring**.

I'm constantly seeking to improve my life as much as I can. I recall the first time I had an in-depth conversation with my mom about my decision to leave the church. She expressed her trust in me, saying, "You've always been on a path to discover the best version of yourself," which really boosted my confidence. The drive to better myself has been within me from birth, but it's not something I can take full credit for. Because I'm fueled to be healthy in every area of my life, I've sought out the best coaches and mentors to get me there.

I want more than anything to truly listen and learn from the best. So, when enough people started telling me the importance of meditation, I was ready and willing. Because of my spiritual background, I was already committed to prayer. I was also good at journaling and reading because these were things I learned in the church. But for some reason meditation did not come easy to me. I literally bought every app, tried every technique, and read a shelf-full of meditation books. I even bought a headset. Didn't work. I couldn't sit still for even 10 minutes. I would just go nuts. Finally, after four years of trying multiple times a week, I now meditate every day for over 20 minutes.

Not only did I begin to feel the benefits of meditation, but the people around me noticed as well. My close friends would say, "You feel calmer. You're much easier to be around. Your energy is so much more inviting now. You seem more grounded." These masculine traits were always things that I wanted to embody, and they only came to me after learning to simply be with myself.

Seeing the huge benefits of making a simple change like a daily meditation, I began to research other habits I could add or remove from my life. Ice baths may get mocked for being trendy, but it's actually so damn powerful. That's why it's so popular! A year ago, I bought a horse trough intending to do ice baths every morning. I didn't fill it once. It seemed like too much effort, and I didn't see the immediate benefits to warrant all the effort.

Most people waste time trying to find the perfect system, supplement, or diet. Well, it's not that complicated—**the best system is the one you'll actually use!** Done is better than perfect. The ice bath wasn't the problem, it was the activation energy required to set it up. I needed to find a system that I would actually do. For me, that system was a $6,000 ice bath that removed all the friction. Now, I use it every day. It's a game-changer. You don't need to buy the most damn expensive thing like I did. What you need to do is find what works for you. It could be as simple as standing in the coldest water your shower can pump out for as long as you can. Maybe there's a freezing cold lake near you. All it takes is the decision to do something you know you'll actually do in the pursuit of achieving your goals.

I had to find what worked for me with meditation as well. After lots of trial and error, I found a meditation that started with verbal guidance and ended with calming music. That's what I needed to relax into the meditation and maintain that state. With that system, I can take out my headphones and stay in my meditation forever if I want to. I also added walking as a way to bring more calm into my life. My coaches kept telling me, "Prioritizing time alone, fitness, and diet is the only way to reach your next level," but I didn't think I had time or space in my life for "self-care." My way of forcing this on myself was getting a dog so I would have to stay home more often and go on walks every day. But again, you don't need a dog, you need a system that you'll follow.

Once you start stacking small wins (meditation, walking, etc.) you can tackle more daunting habits. One of my biggest challenges was to wake up at 7:00 a.m. It's a common goal, right? But I couldn't get myself to wake up before then because I'd stay up late the night before. Like I told you in an earlier chapter, I hacked the system by having one of my members be at my door at 7 a.m. This allowed me to do in-person, one-on-one coaching, but not from behind a desk! Not only did it force me to wake up, but after doing this for over a year, I started going to bed earlier, and now I wake up on my own around 6:00 or 6:30 a.m.!

The best system is the one you're going to use, especially with your health. If you're in a house with young kids or a spouse who likes to bake all the time, you need to find a system that works with your schedule, diet, and priorities. Nothing is impossible and if you desire it enough, you'll make it work. Forking out six grand for something that just causes me pain was not my all-time favorite purchase, but it was the one I needed to make to activate the change.

Speaking of the cost of transforming your lifestyle, I've been wanting to have steak, halibut, and cooked organic veggies every day because of their obvious health benefits. But having it delivered via GrubHub for $55 every single meal was in no way sustainable. I think I did that once. So now, instead of paying over $1,000 a week on food delivery, I pay a friend who helps me meal prep lunch and dinner. Once per week, I hire him for a few hours to cook all my healthy foods for the week. Again, this is yet another way I've hacked the system for my short- and long-term benefit.

By nourishing my body correctly, I'm not hungry and snacking on junk food because I'm filling up on good fats, calories, and proteins. When it comes to health and wellness, done is better than perfect. You don't have to reinvent the wheel or get sucked into somebody else's hamster wheel. Meditation, prayer, journaling, cold bath, affirmations, goal-setting, having a vision board, walking, going to the gym, drinking a gallon of water—I now do all of these things every day. It will take you time to get all these things on point, but you absolutely have to if you have any intention of living a life you're happy to wake up for every single day.

You should not attempt this transformation alone. Find people who are already where you want to be and hire them or observe them.

By reading this book, you're doing just that. Find the people and systems that help you break away from who you are and breakthrough to who you want to be.

Stand for What Is Sacred

At the time of writing this book, what is and is not healthy is a taboo subject. So many people are afraid to approach it, myself included. When I was overweight, I resented people approaching this subject. When I read things from people who had better resources, education, and opportunity than me, it made me defensive. My go-to was to say things like, "Being healthy was not in my genes," or "My childhood diet destroyed my metabolism." When the truth is hard to swallow, we'd rather eat lies.

If you want to make real change, you have no other option but honesty. If you want to survive, let alone thrive, you have to get back to the truth. And the truth is, if you're not taking care of your body, you're not taking care of your health. Your physical health affects every aspect of your life. That's a fact. There's room for appreciating where we're at and for loving your body the way it is. However, you must have the authenticity and integrity to call things as they are.

To be a good man, you must stand for what is good, true, and sacred. You must be willing to be mocked, ridiculed, or delegitimized. The warrior doesn't unsheathe his sword for someone throwing rotten tomatoes in his face. A police officer doesn't arrest someone for being given the bird. In America, you can tell the president to "go to hell," and that's entirely within your rights. But since you're not the kind of person who would do that, that means you're someone who will stand for what is true.

An undeniable truth you must stand for is that you will have a more passionate life if you're healthy. You're going to live a longer, better life if you're healthy. You're going to be able to be with your loved ones more. You're going to have the energy, vision, and courage to dream of (and do!) more extraordinary things. There's a level of life that you can't access if you're not healthy. If you put toxic stuff in, you're going to experience toxic things. But as you feed yourself, surround yourself, and bring goodness to everyone else around you, you're going to cultivate a strength that no one can take away from you.

It was obvious to me that if I'm going to support men becoming the best version of themselves, I had to do my best to live by what I know is true. And there's nothing that will lead to a more purposeful, powerful, and fulfilled life than first being vulnerable, then authentic, and as a result, becoming a man of integrity. A man of integrity is not a man of perfection. He's a man who strives to become a better version of himself and has the vulnerability to be honest when he's fallen short.

Real Talk

There's a confidence that comes when you look in the mirror and you say, "You know what? I earned that." There's a reason why people used to like the idea of having a six pack because they know the effort it takes to earn it. You can't paint it on; you can't just have it; you have to earn it. You can give people money, but you can't give them a six pack. It has to be earned. And the person who is just given money is the biggest fool to think they can just take it. Contemporary movements that openly attack people who are dedicated to fitness as "far-right" or manufacture studies that "prove" gym-goers are narcissistic are just as foolish as the chump who takes handouts and "free" money.

Feeling good about your appearance is not a political statement or a deficiency of character. It's time you block out all the noise of people arguing what a good, healthy man should be, and it's time you become one. You can't fully love yourself, when you allow your health to be less than what it could be. That might be a little taboo to say, but it's true. I say this not from the peak of the mountain top but from someone who's in the trenches. I still have cravings for Burger King Whoppers. I still drink way too many damn Celcius. I drink lots of Coke Zero and bite off the damn straw and chew on it because sometimes, without even realizing it, I can be a sugar-addicted, anxious, distracted, dopamine-seeking, nervous wreck. But I'm seeking progress, not perfection.

To work out like a true warrior, and stop being a damn worrier, you have to undo hundreds of years of your ancestors being conditioned to seek comfort. We've been given access to foods we're just now starting to understand are the reasons for more cancer, more heart disease, and mental disorders than ever recorded in human history. Yet these foods create the cravings that keep us coming back. As long as you're putting in toxicity, your cells are doing all they know to do—ask for more of what made them.

I get it. You're too busy. There are just too many other things that you have to worry about. I have people who are close to me— family, friends, and partners—who get mad at me because they, like most everyone, are just trying to live day to day. They don't have time to think about these things. So, I've second-guessed myself, "Well, does that mean that I shouldn't say these things?" "Should I just eat the damn potato chips to make them feel better?" "Do I drink the blue Rockstar to show myself I'm not perfect?" Hell, no. I'm going to do what I know I should do. I'm not going to keep blaming some past, present, or projected future circumstances. When you know better, you do better.

Stop Trying to Feel Better

Writing this chapter made me uncomfortable. It's not that I don't feel confident in what I'm saying because I know it's accurate. I'm uncomfortable because not all of my actions align with being healthy. I'm a serial phone-checking, task-accomplishing Energizer Bunny. I eat faster than I should. I look at my phone more than I need to. I could spend the rest of this section listing all the things I do that I know aren't great. I've created an incredibly supportive life for myself and others, which requires constant time, energy, and attention, but I've built it mostly via two chemicals: caffeine and dopamine. So how do I make sense of these contradictions?

The reason why speaking on physical health makes me uncomfortable is not because I've figured it all out, but because I'm still figuring it out. I struggle with an immediate sense of anxiety whenever I feel like I'm not being productive, a compulsive relationship with my phone, a craving for cold/fizzy drinks, and so on. Guys like to front like we've always got our ducks in a row, but right now, I'm at the edge of my own imposter syndrome. People think authors write books because we have things figured out, but remember that secret from this book's Intro? Authors write books about what they've tried to master. Did I come out of the womb like The Rock: six-foot-four, with the endurance of a triathlete? No. But I have a willingness to fail in the process of succeeding. That's gotten me pretty damn far, and it'll take you farther than you believe you could go.

The first thing most of us do when we're anxious is go to our phone, go to food, or something else that gives us dopamine. When I was overweight, I was not addicted to food—I was addicted to dopamine. We get addicted to our own hormones, and we're overstimulating ourselves with pleasure.

Educate yourself about what to eat or how to have a more intentional relationship with your phone, but you'll ultimately recognize that the real addiction is within your own endocrine system. However, you can't make the object your enemy. You have to learn to recognize the ritual you've built around the repetitive actions you take. When you reach for your phone, reach for the food, or whatever the behavior is that you want to stop doing, you have to pause the hamster wheel because you know exactly where it's going to take you.

If you never stop to recognize what's happening in your body in the moment of compulsion, you'll never stand a chance to overcome it. When you start to feel anxious, insecure, overwhelmed, or exhausted, pause before you reach for your phone or a coffee. Say aloud, "I feel anxious, and this isn't going to give me what I really want." If you can't commit to that step, then you'll be heading to the fridge, looking at porn, or drinking that damn drink every time.

The answer to addiction is recognizing your true needs and fighting like hell to keep those feeling suppressors away. Here's a secret about life. **It's not about feeling better. What we really want is to feel more.** That's the key. It doesn't matter what you're feeling, what you really need is to feel it more deeply. You've gotta feel it to heal it. Stop trying to feel better. Overeating, taking drugs, going to our phones, watching TV, playing video games, or whatever your vice is makes you feel "better." But that means not feeling what will help you *get* better. Self-awareness is not the same as intelligence. *Intelligence* is the ability to understand information. *Wisdom* is making good decisions because of what you know. But *awareness*, the "Holy Grail" of being an extraordinary human, only increases in direct proportion to how quickly, how deeply, and how often you're aware of what you're actually feeling. The more that you feel, the more aware you are.

Be Strong

Many of the actions relating to our health don't have an immediate impact, good or bad. That's the shitty part about health, it's a slow burn to pain and gain. You may not immediately see the benefits or harms of what you do in the moment, but over time, your decisions catch up to you. That's why you need to identify right now as the person you want to be later.

The big change that completely turned my physical health around was when I started seeing myself as someone who was

190 pounds. Once I identified as someone that was 190 pounds, I could make decisions that were consistent with that kind of person: 190-pound Jimmy does not eat the pancakes instead, he eats steak and eggs; 190-pound Jimmy goes to the gym even when he doesn't feel like it.

On a practical level, you can't set diets and goals that aren't specific and attainable. So, I asked myself, "What do I need to do every day? How many calories does this person have? How much protein does he eat? What kinds of workouts does he do on which days?" The most important thing is to have a vision of yourself and then only live as that person. By acting as if you are that person, you will become that person over time.

The only way to increase in physical health is to make small, incremental changes that you'll actually do. I didn't climb Kilimanjaro in one sprint. But I knew I had a journey to go on, so I committed to the fact that the summit was where I was headed. Hearing that it was a life-or-death thing for Q to make it to the top made me realize there was no option for myself and everyone else. There is nothing that directly impacts your quality of life (or untimely death) more than your diet and physical fitness.

There is a clear connection between physical health and overall integrity. When my health was shit, I was stuck in bad habits. It was a combination of willful ignorance, stubbornness, and avoiding my deep feelings of insecurity, shame, and fear. At that point, I had a choice: make being unhealthy an acceptable identity with tragic consequences or realize that the real challenge is to tap into those deep feelings of fear, shame, and insecurity that even made being unhealthy an option in the first place. Not understanding this choice is what blocks people from doing something where they could fail/feel weak. Awareness of this is what will open you up to living a successful life, full of strength, conviction, and purpose.

I'm not going to tell you to count your macros, your steps, or any of the other 18 billion things that could be perceived as fitness advice.

Although all of those things do help with accountability. I'm going to give you the process I use to help increase my self-awareness and develop a positive self-identity. I know this process will help you as it's helped me. These are the 4 Stages of Evolution: **Resistance, Failure, Resilience, and Growth.**

First up is resistance or pushing back. Some examples of positive Resistance are progressive overload with strength training, doing breathing exercises like breath holds (holding your breath for as long as you can with or without air in your lungs), meditation, swimming, slow and controlled movements with lifting weights, and so on. Negative resistance is pretty obvious—it's being a stubborn jackass instead of being a genuine badass.

If you're doing things right, you're going to want to fail; that's the second stage. Failure is best mitigated through accountability. This means you have to tell someone you're committing to a new lifestyle. This is why you need a mentor, but also friends with the same values. Tell your significant other, coworker, or even your parents. Just tell someone what you're committing to give up. This can be embarrassing if it's something like porn or drugs. But those kinds of behaviors just make it 10 times more important to not stay isolated and have people who can hold you accountable to the new version of yourself. Remember, you don't climb Kilimanjaro in one sprint. And the best way to climb it is with people you love and who love you.

While accountability is essential, you're the only one who can choose to overcome all obstacles. Don't quit at the false summit. Resilience, the third stage, is the hallmark of an extraordinary human. Lots of people have ideas. A few people have amazing ideas. And an even fewer number of people do the work to manifest their ideas into reality.

And finally, comes Growth, the fourth and final stage. Your growth motto is, "Done is better than perfect." Don't forget, the whole point of this life is for it to be enjoyed. Mind you, I didn't say it was to make you feel good. All kinds of stress are good for something. The fight or flight stress response of your sympathetic nervous system is good for keeping you alive. Doing an ice bath, marathon, 10-minute meditation, and deep stretching every single morning are all great forms of stress. Internally shaming yourself, causing yourself to worry you'll never be good enough or have what you really want . . . that's not good stress. That's a recipe for disease. Keep it simple, and remember, it's your responsibility to make a stand for what is sacred.

Yes, I'm talking about you.

You're worth it.

Go get it done.

4

Be Fully Devoted

From LEAKY to SECURE

"It is our decisions, not our conditions that dictate our destiny."
—Tony Robbins

I'M NOT GOING to say any one of these chapters is the most important one. However, this chapter is the one you really need to grasp, understand, and apply for you to truly be a good man. While the last three chapters helped you become more devoted to yourself, now you actually have to apply your new identity into every area of your life.

When I went to Mt. Kilimanjaro, I had the option of taking a helicopter to the top. It would have been a nice, easy ride with great views. But there would have been no Dave Vobora. No Q. No hard-won lessons on the journey to the top. Taking the helicopter down would only be doing it halfway. And I'm not one to half-ass anything. "Coming down the mountain" is 10× more important than summiting the mountain. When you return from a peak experience, the journey home is what prepares you to apply the lessons you've learned. None of it really matters if none of it is integrated.

The way you return to your "normal life" and take action determines the kind of person you are. This hiking metaphor is rock-solid because 75% of all hiking accidents happen on the descent! After making it to the top, seeing the 10,000-foot view, and being on top of the world, as you head home, you're almost guaranteed to slip and fall, and potentially mess yourself up. Paying attention to this chapter will prepare you for the climb AND the descent.

Peak, life-changing experiences without integration are just another form of entertainment. If you're really here to do the damn work to be a good man, you've got to pay attention every step of the way down. Not only do you need to bring every single thing in your life into integrity, but it's also your responsibility to share your life-changing realizations with other people. And **there's no greater way to teach others than by being exactly what you want to see**

in the world. Become a man of integrity, and you won't need to say a word. You won't need to explain or open any eyes because you'll be the living example of what it means to be a devoted and confident man. But watch out! Couple that confidence with tenderness and vulnerability to avoid self-righteousness. There's no bigger turn-off than a guy who thinks he's got it all figured out but doesn't have the humility to actually connect with people in a genuine way.

It's important to avoid the thinking trap that if we could just get everything in order, then, only then, could we live our lives to the fullest. But let's be honest; we're not perfect. We chase after the idea of self-mastery, but really only feel our best in fleeting moments. The daily grind and mistakes loom large over the infrequent "aha moments" where everything makes sense.

When I made it to the summit of Kilimanjaro, after six days of suffering, I had the experience of complete clarity. But it's not uncommon to follow up these life-expanding moments by falling flat on our faces. We're at the top and then suddenly we trip over the rug, or back our car into a grocery cart, or say something hurtful to someone we love. I used to look at these downfalls as epic failures, as proof that I wasn't pushing myself hard enough. These stumbles left me feeling inadequate and disheartened, as if there was some vital life lesson I just wasn't grasping. Without realizing it at the time, I carried around a deep-seated sense of being fundamentally flawed.

But after slipping time and time again, I've come to accept that this is just the gritty reality of being human. While you need to do everything you can to mitigate the risk of twisting your ankle when you come down the mountain, you also need to come to terms with failure. One moment, you're sitting on top of the world, and in the blink of an eye, you're messing up and damaging the most precious things in your life. The key is not to punish yourself, but to strengthen and secure yourself. We're not flawless. We're designed to momentarily grasp the whole picture, try our damnedest to apply it to our life, and be kind to ourselves after we realize we've forgotten what truly matters.

In this chapter, I will going to cover how to get your house in order as you "come down from the mountain." Instead of being leaky with your money, sexual energy, time, and attention, you have to become deeply secure within yourself. You've begun to overcome shame, loneliness, and any kind of self-harm. Your mindset is more inspired and decisive. Your body is getting stronger and you're moving like a warrior. Now it's time to start applying that new identity into every area of your life.

Money Doesn't Satisfy; It Magnifies

When you're in integrity, the universe conspires in your favor. But if you're off by even one degree or tell even one white lie, then things will eat at you. Do this enough and your life begins to feel like random chaos. In business, you might think something's just a little accounting "fix," or "Oh, let's just not tell them about this," but you know that's not the path you want to walk.

I had one unbreakable rule on my real estate team: everyone in the transaction should have all the information they needed to make the best decisions. Hiding nothing and disclosing everything was my only option. It kept us out of trouble, and I never had to worry about anything. When you're in integrity, you don't have to worry about remembering what you said. If you're out of integrity, be it with family or business, you're wasting energy trying to maintain a façade. You're using precious time trying to convince other people that you're something that you're not. Wouldn't you rather use that energy toward harnessing your creativity and building something you're confident in?

Being leaky with your word, your promises, your money, and your sexual energy eats away at whatever you're trying to build, be it a relationship or a business. Eventually, it's going to catch up with you. It always does. It's the karmic rule of the universe. We all know someone who does all the "small" misguided things that add up to a giant challenge in the end. They rob Peter to pay Paul, they're just a little bit dishonest here and they don't follow up there. They make excuses and manipulate people. Since they're out of integrity, the way they make their money and create relationships leaves them incredibly unhappy.

When money is demonized, it's often because the people that get it by being out of integrity are so miserable. It's easy to see why many people associate having money with evil deeds and bad people. But people who have come by money through integrity are the ones that do so much good for the world. They're the ones that truly move the planet forward in the best possible ways.

Earl Nightingale famously said, "Success is the progressive realization of a worthy goal or ideal." You can get rich without being in integrity. But you won't be fulfilled because you weren't pursuing a worthwhile goal. Take a drug dealer, paparazzi, or hell, even a pimp. Even if he's the best in the world at it, he's not going to be fulfilled. No matter what he tries to do or how he tries to convince himself, he's not going to be happy. In the world I want to live in, the goal is not to be rich. The goal is to be extraordinary. The goal is to be fulfilled. That's the real definition of *success*. Tony Robbins put it better than anyone, "Success without fulfillment is the ultimate failure."

Money puts a magnifying glass on your character. If you're happy, you'll be happier. If you're miserable, you'll be more miserable. If you don't have any money and you're miserable, you're likely to think, "Well, if I had money, I wouldn't be miserable." But as soon as you get money, you're still miserable because it magnifies what and who you are. Banking on money to bring fulfillment is a bad investment because you're conditioned to believe, "Shit, I'm supposed to be happy, but I can't even blame it on not having money now!" If you've ever been there like I have, you know it's a low place. An authentic sense of security from within is what creates true financial security.

Similar to financial security, being genuinely self-aware will shift your sexual energy into integrity. Instead of being leaky and spread out all over the place, you'll start to be more attractive, magnetic, confident, and wealthy. It's really gross and off-putting to be leaky. This goes for everyone, not just men. People who are loose with their sexual energy, financial spending, or life force are missing something vital. As a man, when you're leaky, that means you're not being the strong, dependable riverbank that you're meant to be. When that flow comes in, by not being secure, your energy spreads without clear direction. Talking to girls online, spending money where you know you shouldn't, accumulating gadgets and shoes you know you don't need, and all the other silly, boyish things we do when we don't have the wisdom or emotional intelligence to be aware that we're feeling insecure.

A lack of masculine direction will make you incapable of handling the new energy flows as you make changes in your life. This flow could show up as the largest sum of money you've ever produced. Or now that you're dieting and working out, the flow could be more romantically charged. When most men feel a surge of energy, all they know to do is release it somehow, some way. Porn, video games, social media, boats, cars, you name it—we've got millions of ways to feel instant relief.

To really get your house in order, you have to learn to settle into yourself and cultivate your energy, not just throw it all away. Men everywhere need to understand this: your relationship to your sexual energy and money are one and the same. If you have any shame in one area, it will lead to a compensation, or an overcompensation, in the other. One guy could pinch every damn penny he touches but be like a fire hydrant with his life force. Another guy could be 10× more of a miser, but be more sexually locked up than Fort Knox.

Each person is different, but the point remains: if you're out of integrity with one, the other will be insecure, unattractive, depolarizing, and wasteful.

Money Isn't the Root of All Evil . . . Scarcity Is

Beliefs about money come from our family, community, and culture. Most people play within or close to the sandbox they were born into. We have a money barometer that lives in our subconscious that influences all of our behaviors. Therefore, **you make the exact amount of money that you subconsciously believe you deserve**. You likely heard some unfortunate things about money growing up, "money is the root of all evil," or "money doesn't grow on trees," or "we can't afford that." Those words stick in the back of your mind, and without even realizing it, you start to believe that money is scarce.

But that's not true. Money is not scarce. It just isn't. Look around your environment right now, and with your imagination, you can start to see the abundance of money and opportunity all around you. If you want to see it, you will. Or, if you want to keep believing that money isn't everywhere, that's true too.

There are over 22 million millionaires in the United States alone. Almost 7% of all Americans figured out how to be a millionaire and people still try to say it's scarce. If you ever hear that it's impossible to be a millionaire, it will be one of dumbest things you'll ever hear in your life. Have you ever heard that it's impossible to get a master's degree? Roughly the same number of Americans have those. Why is money different? Because money comes with baggage. Most people stay in the same demographic they're born into because it's hard to break out of how they've been programmed. Thankfully, there are simple exercises and things you can do to create a supportive relationship with money.

Consistently evaluating your money barometer is the first step toward a healthy relationship with money. First and foremost is to believe you deserve wealth! Do not say no to money in any capacity. If someone offers to buy me something, I let them. You want money to flow to you. You want to let the universe know that you're deserving of whatever ways you're getting taken care of.

The next step is resetting the benchmark of what $1 million dollars really means. Start with an imaginary $1,000, and pretend you have to spend it. Go online and see what you'd buy to spend the entire $1,000. The next day, you double it. The next day, you double it again and again. Keep doing that for 30 days. By day five, you have to spend $16,000. You might say you'll buy a car or put a down payment on a condo. Eventually, you'll be spending $256,000, $4 million, and beyond. Once you start to see what you'd buy for $4 million, it doesn't take long for you to realize that it's not very much money. You'll go from "I want to be a millionaire one day" to realizing how quickly that money will evaporate.

By the time you get into the millions, you think you're going to buy your dream house. But once you see the house you want, along with all the taxes, upkeep, and expenses, you'll be broke in a few months. You realize for those first few million, you'll stay living in your condo, maybe buy that boat, book a trip around the world, give $1 million to your church, put $500,000 for each child in their college fund, and before you know it, you're out of money again. The reality is, $4 million won't go nearly as far as you once thought.

At one point, I had over $30 million tied up in Nikola Motors stock because I invested in the company prelaunch. I was either making or losing more than a million dollars daily, depending on the stock's performance. Can you imagine how difficult it was to motivate myself to sell houses when I could potentially earn or lose millions in a day? This experience altered my understanding of money and its fluidity.

It's an extraordinary experience to make $15 million in a day as I did on June 9, 2020, and then lose $10 million in a day a few months later. For four months, I thought I had $30 million dollars, worst case $15 million. It was in my account, my shares just couldn't be sold for a few more months. Three months before I could pull any money out, the founder and my former friend, Trevor Milton, was caught for fraud. My shares plummeted to a fraction of what I thought they would be worth. But the real gift of this roller coaster summer was the opportunity to ask myself, "What would I do if money didn't matter?" "What will my life look like when I don't have to worry about money?" "How will my life change?" I was quick to realize that not much would change, except for one thing: I would focus more on my coaching and much less on my real estate.

Then it hit me like a brick to the face, "Why would I not live that life RIGHT NOW if it were sure to be the choice I am going to make when I finally 'have enough money.'" So, I went all in. I figured out how to do exactly what I wanted to do and ended up making more money than when I was selling real estate by helping hundreds of men find healing, purpose, friendship, and community. Since going full-time with We Are The They, I hear countless stories of the changes people are making to make their life better, and I know that I made the right decision. I didn't need an eight-figure exit from my investment to build the exact life I wanted to have.

Learn to Play the Money Game

To succeed in getting your house in order, you have to learn the rules of the money game. Do you truly understand money? If I were to ask you about cap rate, do you know what it means? Or what about an annuity?

Here's a scenario: Let's say you're planning for your retirement and you're considering an annuity as an investment option. An insurance company offers you an annuity where you make a one-time payment of $200,000, and in return, the company will pay you $10,000 per year for the next 30 years. How much money would you receive in total from the annuity over the 30-year period? If you take into account an average inflation rate of 2% per year, how much would the $10,000 you receive in the 30th year be worth in today's dollars? If instead of buying the annuity, you invest the $200,000 in a savings account with an annual interest rate of 3%, how much would that investment be worth in 30 years? Was this hard to follow? If this is stressful or confusing to you, you don't understand the rules of the game. This is your wake-up call to be a student of money.

Once you understand the rules, you can play effectively. For years, I had no idea where my money was going, but I realized that **if I didn't track every dollar, I was going to lose it**. The trick is to value and respect your money enough to keep tabs on it. Don't ever pass over a penny. If you do, you're telling the universe that money isn't important to you. But it does matter; it's a tool to create value in every other area of your life.

Stop Leaking; Start Living

Men who are out of integrity with their money are attracted to those who are leaky with their sexual energy (paying for OnlyFans, porn, strip clubs, etc.). Leaky is attracted to leaky. Toxicity is infectious in every area of life, but especially in regard to sex and money.

There's nothing more gross than a guy that's out of integrity. Many guys are sneaky, Machiavellian manipulators so they can trick you for a little while, but you know when it's happening. It's the guy that talks to your girlfriend any time you're away from her or the old guy that touches her lower back when she walks by. It's the guy at the office who says things that he shouldn't or probes too much on a coworker's sex life. Having leaky sexual energy is where every guy in the history of humankind has gotten in trouble. It's where all toxic masculinity comes from. All toxic masculinity comes from leaky sexual energy. Period.

That's what getting your house in order means. It's where you stop all of the leaks, really check yourself, and evaluate what the heck you're doing. You can't be a man of integrity if your sexual energy is pouring out everywhere. It's even more damaging when this happens with people in positions of power (therapists, bosses, or church authorities). It can completely devastate and wreck people's lives. People who are genuinely secure within themselves are not leaky with their sexual energy. Because of this, they are able to create a lot of safety and healing for people.

Money can also create structure and safety, allowing you to do better in the world. I'll say it again, money is a magnifying glass. If you've done the work to feel deeply secure within yourself, you're going to use your money to give back and help others. If you're leaky, you're going to attract leeches who will literally suck you dry of your finances and life force. Just because they exist doesn't mean they deserve to get all of your time, attention, energy, and resources.

Be Secure

This is not a finance book, but there are basic things you must know about money. If you haven't read MONEY Master the Game by Tony Robbins, Think and Grow Rich by Napoleon Hill, or Rich Dad, Poor Dad by Robert Kiyosaki, I highly recommend them. Each of these books targets a different aspect of increasing your financial integrity. With that foundation, and applying what you've learned from this chapter, you'll begin to understand the game.

Understanding is one thing; doing is another. You have to know where every single one of your dollars goes. After I'd been in real estate for a couple of years, my bank account was nearly empty. I'd made over $400,000 a couple of years in a row, but somehow, I didn't have any money. I thought I was spending $6,000 a month, but since I didn't have a budget, I didn't really know. I hired a bookkeeper and she found I was spending over $20,000 a month. I had money going everywhere and I didn't even know it. I was the leakiest guy in the room. I didn't just have a leak; I had a burst pipe.

Thankfully I started reigning it all in just as the market tanked. By stopping the leaks, I went from running a budget of about $8,000 a month down to $3,500 just to survive because I couldn't sell any houses. What if I didn't get my house in order? My house would have flooded, and I'd have been screwed. It all started by identifying and fixing the leaks.

It's not enough to stop the leaks; you have to start diverting that flow into savings. You need to put six months of savings aside. One of the biggest financial mistakes you can make is to increase your spending as you make more money. Nicer trips, longer vacations, bigger houses, more cars, nicer shoes, nicer clothes, better restaurants, and the hamster wheel never stops. The key to getting wealthy is that as you make more money, you grow in discipline to not let the money leak out. Don't raise your cost of living. Don't constantly expand your lifestyle. What turned around my saving habit was to open a second bank account at another bank. Every single check, I put over 30% of my earnings into this account. Since I couldn't see it, I finally built up those six months of savings. If I saw the money in my account, I would have spent it because I was just beginning to grow in security and integrity.

After a few years, without even missing the extra money, I had saved over $200,000 in this bank account. Because I was more secure, I used that money to buy all my own real estate investment properties, which put me on the path to becoming truly wealthy. Don't touch savings accounts, unless it's to add to them or transfer it into a wise, virtuous, and intentional investment. Don't be like most people who just raise how much they're spending when they start to make more money. If you can keep your same budget and live the same lifestyle for a couple of years, then all of a sudden, you'll have more potential for actual wealth creation. When you invest your saved money wisely, meaning constantly and consistently, everything else in your life will feel and become more secure.

This bears repeating, your money and sexual energy are linked. When you look to material things or superficial relationships to fill a void, you're simply looking to feel more than your baseline. We want to feel! But when you use external things to generate or mask feelings, it drops your baseline further and further toward despair. If you're only making withdrawals from your life force and depositing it into nothing, maybe a sock, towel, or in the shower, that means the sleep you're getting, the food you're eating, and the water you're drinking is being wasted on a bad investment. The girls on your phone don't know who you are. They don't care about you. They just need your time, attention, and money to feel an overwhelming sense of worthiness. What you get from it is worse than nothing. It leaves you in debt to yourself. It leaves you exhausted, disconnected, and insecure. When you feel secure within yourself, you're not going to look to money, women, or anything else to reach a healthy baseline.

One of the biggest issues I see today is how normalized it is to pay for adult content. It's a multi-billion-dollar industry. It's also controversial to say that it's destructive because it could be perceived as a judgment toward women doing something financially empowering. Sure, it may be a way to make money, but the entire industry only exists because there are men, completely out of integrity, who desire it in the first place. Prostitution is often referred to as "the world's oldest profession." It has been recorded in nearly every civilization in history, from ancient times to the present day. But we've reached a level of desensitization that not only do we condone it, but we actively promote it.

As a man of character, not only should you purge yourself of this toxicity, but actively create an environment of safety so that toxic behaviors with money or sex aren't even an option. The exchange between a sex worker and a patron often originates from the same place—not being secure within themselves so they need to use another for short-term rewards. But by doing this, consensual or not, there is a complete disconnection to who you truly are. It's not innocent. It's corrosive. It's completely out of integrity, and it's a deep, deep, issue. I've seen firsthand the destruction this creates on both sides of the transaction.

As you get your house in order, remove all the leaks, cultivate your energy, save and invest your money wisely, and share your wealth. The security you'll feel within yourself will attract better lovers, better friends, better opportunities, and more things that set your soul on fire.

Bonus Section

Abraham Maslow was an influential psychologist who is best known for creating the Hierarchy of Needs, a way to understand our innate human needs. For this bonus section, I'm giving you a sneak peek into a process I share with members of We Are The They. You'll discover where you currently stand with your finances—numbers that will be defined by who you truly are, free from childhood, learned, or cultural expectations. This new, authentic baseline comes from understanding Survival, Stability, Success, and Significance:

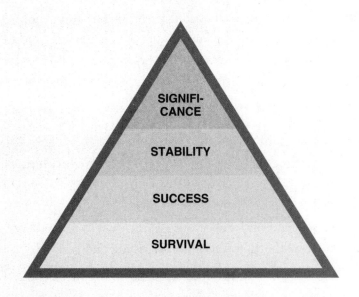

SURVIVAL

This is the number you MUST make to keep your car from being repossessed, your lights on, and your rent/house paid. These are your fixed expenses (these are the same each month): $___

STABILITY

This is the number you need to make to put money in savings for cover emergencies and to start to build wealth (tires, new fridge, savings), and so on: $___

SUCCESS

This is the number that YOU define as *success*. Some decide this is a salary for being in the Top 1–2% in their career, company, or team. Others define it as the number that allows you to have one to five years of income in the bank and your insurances are all up to date (life insurance, health insurance). It could be the number you need to be debt free and to keep the lifestyle you enjoy and money for vacations, college funds, and replacing cars/appliances without moving back into the Survival or Stability zones: $___

SIGNIFICANCE

This is the amount that would blow YOUR mind. This is the amount of money that would allow you to continue in Success (saving, building wealth, and investments) AND allow you to give back from your abundance of time, energy, and money without affecting your existing success: $___

If money is tight, break it down to a monthly figure for each category. How much money do you need to make every month to be in Survival, Stability, or Success? Be aware of whose voice is talking in your head as you evaluate these numbers for your life. Many people do not succeed and move out of Survival or Stability if their parents never made that much money. Some people choose smaller numbers because they are afraid of what family or friends (who have shitty beliefs about money) will think of them. These are YOUR numbers for the life YOU would love, not anyone else's.

Answer these questions:
- What is preventing me from moving from Survival to Stability?
- What actions can I take to eliminate those obstacles?
- What is preventing me from moving from Stability to Success?
- What actions can I take to eliminate those obstacles?
- What beliefs do I need to have, change, or strengthen to take action and eliminate those obstacles?
- What is preventing me from moving from Success to Significance?
- What actions can I take to eliminate those obstacles?
- What beliefs do I need to have, change, or strengthen to take action in order to eliminate those obstacles?

If we want to improve our financial security and success, we need to evaluate whom we spend the most time with. Are they financially astute? Do they seek ways to improve their current status in life? Do they encourage me to grow and develop this area of my life? If not, you need to level-up your peer group and focus on those who elevate your game.

5

Be There . . . But *Really* Be There

From AVOIDANT to PRESENT

"Wherever you are, be there."

—Ron Hammond

FOR YOUR LIFE to be great and to be in the circles you want to be in, you have to do new things or do familiar things in a new way. As Thomas Jefferson said, "If you want something you've never had, you must be willing to do something you've never done." Everybody wants to have *that* life. Everybody wants to be in *those* circles. However, the things that will prevent you from getting there are not gigantic hurdles, they're tiny habits. You don't show up on time, your breathing is a little bit off when you work out, or you make mistakes and don't correct them. The problem is becoming accustomed to who we are and how we are. That's fine if you're dialed in, but if not, you need to learn to get out of your own way. Getting out of the way means getting into the way of presence. You have to become deeply present so you're able to see every situation, every opportunity, and every experience with fresh eyes, an open mind, and a heart of service.

When I started connecting with successful leaders and mentors, I was curious how they could give me so much time and attention. I would ask them all the same question, "Why me?" and a clear pattern of feedback emerged. One mentor, in particular, a multibillion-dollar fund manager, helped me see the value I was bringing to the table. He got me into working with Operation Underground Railroad, but it wasn't clear why he'd picked me from the hundreds of others lined up to go undercover. "Why?" he said, "Because every single thing I gave you to do, you just showed up and did it. And you did it better than expected." He went on to say that I did things better than he would have done, and that's why he wanted me to be around.

Now that I'm as busy as he was, I understand why it's so valuable to have people in my life that just get shit done. If I don't have to follow up, I don't have to worry, and it's done well. That level of presence and personal empowerment allows everyone to have a more passionate work life.

So many people can't get out of their own way. It's invaluable to do what you say you're going to do, to be on time, to look like you belong there, and to do things well. This is the easy stuff, table stakes, but some people want to skip over the basics and head right to being "the man." My friend Andy Frisella takes this to heart in how he runs his business. If you don't wipe out the sink after you wash your hands, you'll get fired. He will literally fire you because he believes that how you do anything is how you do everything. When I had him on my podcast, he was giving me a tour of his building, and every single weight in their weight room was exactly lined up where the number was right in the middle. Everyone knows what's expected and they know what to expect if they don't. Show up or go home because how you do anything, is how you do everything.

You Don't Live to Work. You Work to Live.

Business should be done in a way that fulfills you and brings you joy. If your professional life is wearing you down, it will impact your family life. Likewise, an unstable family life will affect your business. By choosing to enjoy your work, you'll prevent toxicity from leaking into other aspects of your life, impacting the people, relationships, and lifestyle that truly matter to you. At the end of the day, work isn't everything. What you need is a sense of fulfillment and purpose. Sometimes, that comes from work, while other times it's derived from activities outside work. Either way, it's important to work passionately so that it doesn't take away from the fulfillment you derive from the rest of your life.

If you despise your job, you're spending 35% to 45% of your day unhappy and compiling stress. Given the few hours you have outside of work, catching up becomes a difficult task. That's why you need to find a way to enjoy work—not necessarily loving every aspect of your job but appreciating the virtue of being devoted to your work. Like a farmer who absolutely loves getting their hands dirty in the field in spite of the toll on their body. Or for me in real estate, it was the love of achieving results and building a business despite the daily grind of making calls. I definitely didn't envision it as my dream job, but I fell in love with delivering excellence to my clients. I knew that when they hired me, they genuinely got the best option.

Just because you love playing video games doesn't mean you should get paid to play, or that you should be a professional hunting guide because you love to hunt. If you do that, you'll have fallen for the concept of following your passion, and you'll probably never spend a second hunting in your free time. Learning to love hard work, regardless of the task, is like going to the gym—it's strenuous, but enjoyable. We love the gym because we know we're developing, and the post-workout feeling is fulfilling.

Many people mistake having a passionate work life with loving what they do every day. To me, having a passionate work life means going to bed feeling satisfied because you've given every day your all, regardless of the circumstance. When the real estate market tanked, I was managing almost 50 listings, but no homes were selling. People would ask me how I was managing, and I'd think, "I'm grinding and I'm hanging on. What's the alternative? To be a loser?" Not being successful wasn't an option. Even if the results weren't as desired, knowing that I put in an honest, hard day's work was all the satisfaction I needed to get through that tough time. There was chaos all around: colleagues leaving the office, people in deep depression, friends losing their life savings, houses going under, people being evicted—it was intense. Despite all this, I felt deeply satisfied because I was putting in my full effort every single day.

Learn to Lead

My do-whatever-it-takes mindset did have some unintended consequences, though. I was getting things done, but I was taking on way too many responsibilities. What had gotten me into *those* rooms and living *that* life was now harming me and the people around me. I had to learn to decrease my responsibilities while increasing my responsibility. By delegating tasks to others who would benefit and learn from them, I alleviated stress and improved as a responsible leader. But delegating requires finding those people you can trust to nail things and be excellent without you looking over their shoulder.

No matter your current situation, you're sure to encounter career/business problems that will be difficult to solve. You could be the CEO, just starting your business, or a new employee; it DOES NOT MATTER. We all face similar challenges and knowing how to navigate them is crucial to have a passionate work life. It's the job of an empowered person to figure out how much they'll help someone figure something out versus having them figure it out. Our self-confidence is improved when we get something on our own. A good leader gives enough direction that the task is manageable, but not without difficulty. A good leader leaves room for a challenge. If there's no pressure to find an answer, things won't get done or the work will land back in your lap.

I thought I was helping people by taking on extra responsibilities. Years later, the people I was "helping" started resenting me because it stunted their growth. I thought I was doing a favor for my real estate team by taking on the expenses and being in charge of everything. But at the end of the day, I didn't do a good enough job helping them become their own leaders. I didn't even know there was resentment built up until after I turned over my real estate team.

Watching their business grow once they left my team was a humble reminder that I was probably getting in their way more than helping them grow. It was my own fault for not holding them to a higher standard of what the expectation would be on my team. I avoided conflict and wasn't really present to their needs or my own.

Top performers want to associate with others of the same caliber. NBA free agents often join teams with other A players, because they know it's exhausting to be the only one. But it's just as exhausting to put up with mediocre teammates. If you allow those who are careless, tardy, or incompetent to stick around, your A players get frustrated and may leave. As a leader, your job is to surround yourself with A players exclusively. Keep them around by ruthlessly replacing your underperformers.

As a leader, I've learned to identify individuals with talent, place them in the right position, and hold them to a higher standard than they would hold themselves to. In my real estate business, I really struggled to hold newer agents accountable. If a team member said they'd make 20 calls that day and didn't, there were no repercussions. I was not a strong enough leader as I allowed the new team members to underperform, preventing their growth, progress, and earnings. My team stagnated and never performed to its potential because I found it too much of a hassle. What I really needed to do was establish higher standards. I remember telling them, "I can't want this for you more than you do," but what I should have done was fire a few people who weren't committed to making the calls and reporting their numbers. They would have appreciated it as well. Allowing them to grow in ways they couldn't otherwise, even if uncomfortable for a time. I'm now more intent than ever on setting high expectations for the people I work with. It's more honest, less work down the road, and creates a more passionate work environment for everyone.

Strategically Unbalanced

There's a myth that we should be balanced in all areas in life, especially when it comes to your career. But anyone that has done something remarkable in this life has done so by being strategically unbalanced. Let me explain. If you want to be the greatest father or entrepreneur that you can possibly be, you will have to focus and give a certain project or responsibility everything you've got. Without being strategically unbalanced, we'll find ourselves lacking in most categories rather than succeeding. You have to put in all of your time, all of your attention, and all of your energy into one specific goal if you want to accomplish something extraordinary. Once you have reached a certain level in that specific area, that's when you can step back and see where you have other gaps. If you're always trying to live a balanced life, you will never get ahead. You will always be just a bit behind in all categories as long as you don't give one your full focus to raise your threshold.

If you're still living paycheck to paycheck and stressed over money, your quality of life is absolutely going to go down until you can earn more. You have to get strategically unbalanced in your life and focus on earning above all else. Sadly, most people don't even know what it means to work hard. I once had a guy shadow me for one day, and he was literally passed out halfway through the day. He was just watching me work and he was so tired, he couldn't handle it. If he wanted a fraction of the lifestyle I had, he would have to become unbalanced compared to his comfort zone.

My close friend Justin Prince is one of the top network marketers in the nation. He's a huge success. People admire him and want to be where he is in life, but they don't know what it took to get there. When he first started out, I remember being in a random Korean restaurant in the worst part of town sitting in the back kitchen trying to explain his product to the owner. It was 10:00 p.m., closing time for the restaurant, and we didn't speak their language. He was up against impossible odds and not letting up. I'll never forget thinking to myself, "One day, this dude's gonna have so much money and success, and people are gonna be like, 'Wow, look at him, lucky guy' and I'm going to remember this moment."

At that time, Justin was driving a beat-up car and was just cutting his teeth in the business. He worked so hard, while his wife was raising their newborn and other young kids. By the time his kids were nine, he was earning millions. Now, he's the top person in his field nationwide. What's more, he enjoys all the time in the world with his family, doing whatever they want to do. If you look at his social media, he's there with his kids every day. To achieve this, he put in so much time and made enormous sacrifices. He was strategically unbalanced, but at the right time and in the right way.

But here's where people really mess up. They hear what I'm saying and say, "Oh yeah! I'm going to be strategically unbalanced!" They head to the office for 80 hours and just twiddle their thumbs. Realtors are famous for this. They go to the office saying they're going to put in all this hard work, and they sit there, fumble their papers around, make a few calls, jump on the internet, and check a few homes. Next thing they know, it's lunch time. They go to lunch with other realtors who they're never going to sell a house to, and waste time talking about sports, politics, or whatever it might be. By the time they get back to the office, it's 1:30, and it takes another half hour to get back into the grind. Maybe they work hard for two or three hours, go show a house, and the next thing you know, the day is over. In their minds, they "put in" a 10-hour day, but really only worked a few hours.

The difference between successful and unsuccessful people is that successful people have merely learned to do the things that the unsuccessful people don't want to do. When I was in the office, I was very strategic and the other realtors in my office always thought I was standoffish. It wasn't that; I was there to work. If I wasn't going to be working, I wanted to be with my friends, I wanted to be with my family, I wanted to be on a date, or be on a vacation. Strategically imbalanced does not mean working 80 hours a week. What it means is: **when you're there, you're freaking there. You're dialed in, and you're doing the job the way it needs to be done.** Instead of faking 80 hours, just put in a real 40 or 50 hours of hard work and you'll be massively successful.

You know if you're doing the hard work. You just know. You don't have to try and fool anyone because then you're just fooling yourself. I know the difference when I just tell myself I'm working hard today versus pounding phones, making hard calls, making tough decisions, and being really focused. When your cell phone is off or it's in another room, you're writing the report, making the marketing strategy, or building out the business plan, you know when you're dialed in versus just letting life pass you by. Avoidance is never going to make your home life better, expand your business, or grow your bank accounts.

The Hidden Dangers of Living a Safe Life

While I've had my share of ups and downs, one thing I've learned not to do is live a safe life. That doesn't mean I'm reckless. A "safe" life means living within a certain known world that keeps you feeling secure, but really, it's just a way to avoid doing hard things. It takes real courage to be fully present with ourselves, our significant others, children, employees, or friends. Alcohol, food, and entertainment make for nice social lubricants, but they don't usually bring us closer together. Doing the expected you'll feel safe, but you'll be stagnant.

What people don't realize is that what they're feeling is familiarity, not safety. True safety is earned. It's worked for. It's putting forth extra effort to create new opportunities, new experiences, and a chance for something better, greater, and more alive. The most dangerous things lurk in the static of constantly seeking out safety rather than living freely. Safety and freedom are one and the same. One person could say, "I didn't feel safe to say what I thought," while another person could say, "I didn't feel free to say what I thought." The one speaking of safety is inherently coming from a weaker place than someone who didn't feel free. This is important to recognize, even though it may seem like a trivial difference. Why? Because the perspective you have on your experiences is what determines your reality. The person who didn't feel safe is likely to keep feeling that way until someone else gives them that sense of safety, and only then do they feel free. The person who didn't feel free will likely not return to that place, and instead find people whom he does feel free around. Or, learning from that experience, he'll know he has the freedom to speak his mind regardless.

This example highlights the subtle ways we play it safe. Look at your life and take notice of any and all ways you're playing it safe. What are you missing out on because you've been telling yourself the same story? What are you hiding from in fear of being in danger? If you want to go deep on this subject you can check out my book *You End Up Where You're Heading: The Hidden Dangers of Living a Safe Life*. You'll find dozens of inspiring stories and a simple framework to move from a "safe," unfulfilling existence into a life fulfilled.

Avoiding hard work in your professional and personal life is a recipe for losing it all. I've never been concerned about my finances or my career because I have one key skill: I know how to work hard. I have confidence because I am my own asset. In one way or another, I know I can provide, and this belief empowers me to keep moving forward in life. My worst-case scenario? I could always return to making seven figures in real estate or high six figures selling meat door-to-door. Once I realized that I was the asset, I gained true confidence.

This is why many people stay in jobs they dislike—they haven't done the work to prove to themselves they can succeed elsewhere. They stick to a safe life because the risk of pursuing what they truly want feels too daunting. Launching your passion project, starting your own business, or even taking a major trip can seem intimidating when you worry it might financially cripple you. Not knowing if you can provide afterward keeps people from taking these leaps. Instead, they play it safe.

You should never fear losing your job if you're providing more value to the business or marketplace than what you're getting paid. If you bring value, job security isn't an issue. The only risk of being fired is if you're not contributing more than your compensation. As my mentor, Mike Ferry, often said, "A person's income is directly proportional to the value they bring to the economy." An NFL quarterback earns a huge salary because only a handful of people can do that job at that level. I know it may not be popular to say, but for jobs like teaching school, the reality is there are hundreds of thousands of individuals who can perform the basic responsibilities, hence the lower pay. However, if you're a top-notch, elite school-teacher, you'll find ways to earn more through mentorship, speaking, writing books, or private tutoring.

There are necessary roles in our society—nurses, for instance—that are performed by many, so they don't receive higher pay. Yet, in today's times, a full-time plumber can make several hundred thousand dollars a year. Fewer people know how to do it now compared to before, making it a high-paying job. Look at the current salary of a UPS driver as one example. The principle is clear: we are paid proportionately to the value we provide to the marketplace and how easily we can be replaced. Anthony Davis, considered one of the greatest NBA power forwards of all time, earns $45 million a year. Why? Because very few people on Earth can perform at his level. As long as you're not playing it safe, you won't stay stagnant with professional success.

Conclusion

My political leanings are shaped by how I believe people are best helped. The challenge in politics is that those on the left believe we improve lives by providing what individuals need, while those on the right argue that everything must be earned. The truth likely lies somewhere in between. But one thing is certain: self-confidence is gained when you achieve something difficult, build something, or earn something. It comes from an overwhelming supply of evidence that you can do hard things.

Yes, there are those who genuinely need assistance who can't do it on their own. The issue is that we're applauding the first-order effects and ignoring the second and third. While providing for their needs may seem good on paper (first order), it can rob individuals of the self-confidence that comes from accomplishment, the feeling that breeds fulfillment and happiness (second and third order). Earning your college degree means a lot more when you know the sacrifices you made to get it. Despite the societal challenges that it might pose, there is a sense of achievement and confidence that comes from knowing you went out and did that.

Those who are liberal leaning, while certainly not fools, have big hearts but may be misguided in their approach to helping others. Meanwhile, conservatives would benefit greatly with a little more empathy rather than solely advocating for self-reliance. A balance is needed, and there is room for more empathy and giving, but people need to earn their accomplishments. There are three things that must be earned, not given—a healthy body, loving relationships, and a peaceful mind. These things can't be bought; they must be earned. You can't purchase friendships or meaningful relationships. You can't achieve a peaceful mind without putting in the effort, and maintaining a healthy body requires work. The most important aspects of life bring the most happiness precisely because they need to be earned.

The only way to achieve anything is by being fully present to your life, moment to moment. This means being strategically unbalanced to reach new levels of success. Being strategically unbalanced should also extend to decompression; prioritizing rest, regeneration, and active recovery. Whether you're working hard or resting hard, really be there. If you're helping your daughter with her homework, don't scroll through X (formerly Twitter). If you want to have a daughter one day, don't spend every night playing video games, thinking one day a queen will walk into the front door of your smelly apartment and be ready to start a life with you. You have to put in extraordinary effort into your personal and professional life to experience nonordinary things.

Being strategically unbalanced does not require pitting two good things against each other. I've heard fools say things like, "You can't be a successful businessman and a good father." Bullshit. The better businessman you are, the more present a father you're able to be.

Being successful in your business gives you the option of being a present father, but it doesn't guarantee it. Take for example a friend of mine who was the No. 1 commercial real estate agent in the country. He was putting together a deal with a developer and a tech owner near my home in Utah. I happen to be friends with both parties, so he asked me to join them on his private plane to visit Google and Microsoft, and create goodwill. As we toured these buildings, he said, "Jimmy, I haven't seen my kids in a week." All I could ask was, "What's it all for? If you can't even see your kids, I don't get it." He responded, "You know, Jimmy, I just worked so hard to build it up. I don't want to let any of it go." This guy has his own helicopter, he's got his own private planes, and has his name on half of the buildings sold in Utah. He was incredibly successful in his business, but I felt nothing but sadness for him. Even at the top of the top, you still have to make the decision if you're going to live to work or work to live.

It was crystal clear to me that I wouldn't trade places with him for anything in the world. There was no part of me that coveted his life. He'd been trapped by his own success, unable to let anything go. His family life collapsed shortly after. He ended up getting a divorce, and while he's remarried now, the damage was done.

The only ones who'll remember your long hours are your kids, not your boss or your clients. And trust me, it won't be a positive memory of how hard dad worked. At the end of the day, it's those whom matter most who bear the brunt of your choices. Remember this when working toward your goals. The key word in strategically unbalanced is *strategic*. This means being present to your responsibilities. This means increasing your personal responsibility. This means being a man of integrity. This means not avoiding but actively pursuing. So be there, but really be there, wherever you are.

A good way to bring more clarity and passion into your life is doing a quarterly in-depth review. Where are you off? How's your family life? How is your key relationship or your romantic partner? How are your friends? How's your work, and how are your finances (which are two very different things)? How's your spiritual life? How's your mental life?

When something isn't aligning, simply concentrate more on that area. This is how you achieve a balanced life. It's not about trying to allocate an equal amount of time to everything daily—that's ineffective and will only lead to burnout. If you're determined to get something done, you have to commit massive action toward it. By reevaluating where you're putting this enormous dedication quarterly, you'll find balance in life, not because you're treating everything equally but because you're giving 10 times the effort to one thing at a time. This is the key to living a passionate life. No one else can or will do it for you. The world needs you to create value through your business. Your family needs you to show up in full presence. You need to show yourself what you're capable of, and you need to start right now.

You know what you need to do.

Go do it.

6

Be a Man

From SUPPRESSED to CONNECTED

"The ultimate measure of a man is not where he stands in moments of comfort and convenience, but where he stands at times of challenge and controversy."

—Martin Luther King Jr.

IN 2016, I went to the Tony Robbins Date With Destiny event. Over the course of those six days, everything about my life changed. One of the most memorable events was a workshop to understand masculine and feminine energy. To begin, he said, "All right, we're going to have 30 women come up to the stage. They're going to dance, and everyone's going to vote by cheering for which one's the most feminine! Okay?" The women went on stage and started dancing, one by one. The ones whom everyone could tell really embodied their feminine got the loudest cheers. He picked the top three winners, and the women returned to their chairs. Then, Tony said, "Now, I want 30 men to volunteer to come up. They're going to dance, and we're going to see who's the most masculine!"

Well, lucky for me, I had been working with a guy that taught attraction, including how to hold myself, and even dance, as a man. He showed me that when at a dance club, masculine men shouldn't be dancing all over the place, but rather, hold a strong frame, move in a steady way, and just jive in rhythm with the music. The first thing I thought was, "Hell, yeah. I know how to win this." Without hesitation, I started walking up. I was feeling pretty damn good. You should have heard my inner dialogue, "Oh, yeah, I'm gonna win. I know exactly how to do this. I got this."

The music starts and some guys rip their shirts off, humping the floor, and doing the absolute most. And then, when it's my turn, I'm just dancing with the music like a confident, masculine guy would in a club. Without a doubt, I thought I was going to win. The crowd started cheering for each one of the guys, and sure enough, I got one of the loudest cheers for being the most masculine man. I was about to walk off the stage, feeling pretty damn good about myself.

And then, right on cue, Tony said, "Okay! Great! So, do you want to know who the most masculine man up here is?" Everyone was curious, and I was thinking he's for sure going to say it's me. I couldn't have been more wrong. "None of them are because a masculine man would never get on a stage trying to seek the approval of a bunch of random strangers." He got me. He got me so good. I just smiled, put my head down and just walked off in shame. But amid the embarrassment, I realized, "Oh, my hell. He's so right. This is so good. I needed this. I've been wrong about being masculine my entire life."

Does this mean men shouldn't dance? Hell, no. Every man on the planet should be able to feel confident and comfortable enough in his own skin to dance. But no real man, embodying true masculinity, would ever go up on a stage, seeking the approval from strangers. Some may think that there's a beauty in the vulnerability of going up on stage and being seen. But what was the reason I was up there? Was it real vulnerability? Was I being courageous? Was I confidently allowing myself to be seen? It was ego, plain as day. It's very common to mistake ego as vulnerability. We think we're being vulnerable, but really, we're doing it for selfish gain.

In this chapter, I'm not going to waste any time explaining or instigating arguments about what a good man is or isn't. For the men who are here for authenticity, the women reading this to know what to look for in a man, or a teen absorbing key insights to help mold themselves into a strong yet tender-hearted man, this book, and especially this chapter, is for you.

We're living in divisive times. Toxicity is all around us. Many men feel wrong for just being a man. Social movements, news media, and the entertainment industry have been sowing seeds of separation, confusion, and division. Does toxic masculinity exist? Yes. Is masculinity toxic? Absolutely not.

While at that same Date With Destiny event I just described, I also found and defined my life's purpose. I want to share it with you now. It's my ethos, my mission, and my compass: "The purpose of my life is to share my tremendous love with all of God's children, bringing happiness to others through my playful soul and by being an example of living an extraordinary life." The process of discovering my purpose wasn't smooth. I was infected with toxicity in almost every area of my life. But, after learning some painful but essential lessons, like getting up on that damn stage and dancing for a bunch of strangers, I was able to begin to see myself for who I truly am. Now that I know what it truly is to be a good man, it's who I strive to be every single day.

Masculinity Is Not Toxic, but It Is Infectious

Toxic masculinity is a real thing, but major problems arise when people try to make masculinity toxic. Remember what I said in Chapter 4? Leaky sexual energy is one of the most common causes of toxic masculinity. But no man is fundamentally toxic. Every man is capable of goodness. Many of us have toxic behaviors, but we ourselves are not toxic. Making men the villain may create a sense of safety and solve a problem in the short-term. But it also makes good men, who are living misguided lives, more lonely, more isolated, more suppressed, and more disconnected.

Toxic masculinity is associated with the negative conduct of some men within our society, but it just further separates all of us from true safety and true freedom. Masculinity is not naturally good or bad as some may believe; it depends on the culture in which it exists. Masculinity is not the problem, and in fact, we need more of it. We need the kind of masculinity that wants to open a door for a woman, give up a seat on a bus, or work hard to provide for his family. We need men to be brave and take the right kind of risks. We need people who are unafraid to compete in the pursuit of something noble, have the desire to win, and are able to deal with loss in a manageable way. We all instinctively know what positive presentations of masculinity look like, regardless of whatever narrative, agenda, or contemporary social movements want the mainstream to believe.

For the last 75 years, through movies and marketing, society culturally promoted and boosted the damaging glorification of the lone wolf, the individual, and the man who didn't need anybody. This planted seeds that men needed to suppress their emotions to be the hero. Inherently, that culture produced some men who lack empathy and think violence is the answer. At the time of writing this book, society is promoting the weak man as being a safe man. Most contemporary ideas of "self-love" (which isn't an authentic love of one's true self) have convinced men that having a "dadbod" is normal, sexy, even. But when I speak of a weak man, I'm not saying physically.

The most dangerous man is one that is weak emotionally and spiritually. Why? A strong man says, "There is a great chance that I will defeat you in anything we compete at, but, if you win, I will accept it and learn from my failure." The coward thinks, "I will never let my pride be broken. If I get in a fist fight, and it's possible I'll lose, I'll just pull out a knife!"

Toxic masculinity is bad behavior that's a result of the environment in which men have been mixed up in. If you take these same men and put them in an environment that teaches respect, kindness, and love, they will behave in honorable, virtuous, and loving ways. This is called Social Connectedness. It's the antidote to the suppression most men experience. Suppression of emotions, dreams, ideas, sexual energy, vulnerability, and so on will only lead to more dangerous actions through misguided men.

It's time we honor the sacrifices men make every single day. Statistically, men work longer hours, have higher levels of stress, and are not eating correctly. We are seeing a massive drop in sperm count and low testosterone levels due to toxins in our food that can result in low sex drive, erectile dysfunction, tiredness, hair loss, the defeat of muscle, raised body fat, temper swings, and the list goes on. These issues stem from the fact that men still don't feel comfortable discussing their problems or seeking help, which is based on the false belief that strong men don't cry or discuss their emotions. It takes a strong man to open up and be vulnerable when he's been taught the opposite all his life.

Instead of encouraging men to be strong, responsible, and deal with issues head-on, men are softer in their resolve than ever yet more hardened in their heart. From a young age, we prevent them from rough play and hand out medals when they come in last. Healthy families and societies need strong men who can lead. And in a world full of evil, we need brave men to stand up and fight for what's right and protect the ones and the things we love. That's the responsibility that comes with being a man. That's true masculinity.

The biggest part of being a truly masculine man is knowing how to express and be connected to your emotions in a healthy way. It's being a protector of loved ones, but not controlling them. It's being a provider, but not using that as leverage or power. It's being confident and sure of yourself, but not seeking out or trying to get approval of others. An embodied man is not trying to create a façade or an image, nor does he live for the approval of others. Masculinity is getting your house in order, being self-reliant, and being vulnerable, authentic, and in integrity. Most importantly, it's being connected to a community that brings out the best in you and putting in the work to have strong friendships.

Self-Reliance Is Not Doing It All on Your Own

In "Self-Reliance," Ralph Waldo Emerson proposed that for a man to truly be a man, he must follow his own conscience and do his own thing. Essentially, do what you believe is right instead of blindly following society. Written in 1841, this essay is more relevant than ever.

However, being capable, having useful skills, and living a unique life is only meaningful if it's able to be shared with others. The lone wolf isn't a healthy or sexy archetype anymore. There's nothing more masculine than being a part of a pack of brothers and sisters, people who will be there when you need them, and surrounded by countless mentors who will be your "Dave Vobora."

However, as men, we are often the sole factor for negatively impacting our growth. We can always find a thousand things to blame, but one day, you'll look at yourself in the mirror and know you're the one who's in charge of every decision you make. Your decisions, if done with courage and consideration of impact, will create a life that is one-of-a-kind but also relatable. You will build self-reliance and self-trust, and avoid conformity or falling into the same traps of misguided men.

Here are three traits of self-reliance:

- Thinking freely.
- Embracing yourself.
- Striving toward your goals, fearlessly.

By combining these three traits, we, as men, become truly unstoppable. This allows us to not depend on others, but to rely on the community around us to grow. Developing self-reliance isn't an easy task. But it is the best way to not get sucked into the toxic times we're living in. We are constantly challenged by the government, media, and even our peers that it's "impossible" to achieve the three preceding traits. But these tests only develop your ability to be compassionate, curious, and confident.

Someone who compares themself to others, belittles others (and themself), and builds up armor to shield themself from pain, but still claims self-reliance, is not self-aware. If anyone tells you they are numb, that's not really what's going on. Being numb is an excuse. What they are is armored, usually because of some past hurt that they haven't had the courage, awareness, or space to heal. Our parents and grandparents' generations are textbook examples of this. That's why "embracing yourself" is the most important example I can give you. It's what will help you keep your bearings, keep you humble, and keep you loving.

This Is the New Masculinity

Growing up in the 1980s and 1990s was an exciting time. Our parents were raised by a generation that fought in World Wars and felt the Cold War's pressure for over 40 years. They knew all about hard work, community, and sacrifice. They didn't have the luxury of fighting about which gender could use which bathroom, or whether or not marijuana was good or bad for the body; they were too worried about putting food on the table and trying to stay out of the next military conflict. Because of their tough upbringing, our parents also had a hard shell around them. From what I've gathered, they didn't want to, they had to, to survive.

As a kid, I remember watching grown men self-destruct and lose their temper. Most of my coaches told me things like, "Suck it up!" or "Don't be a little bitch!" We grew up on movies that taught us it was unmanly to show weakness and fell in love with lines like, "There's no crying in baseball!" I'm grateful for these strong men. Strong men protect us from the wolves that will tear us down if we aren't careful. My mentors taught me hard work, self-reliance, and how to work through adversity. However, I've come to realize there's much more to being a man, and that it's a gift to have the time, space, and opportunity to explore more aspects of myself than they could.

On my second day of a two-year mission to Mexico, I had a life-changing experience. I was homesick, lost, confused, sad, and struggling. I was in a tough spot, and to make matters worse, my companion didn't speak English, and I didn't speak Spanish. I remember having my monthly sit-down with the president of the mission, and he asked me how I was doing. Trying to be honest and looking for support, I told the truth, saying I wasn't doing well. He responded by slamming his desk, "Damnit, Rex, I don't want any sissies in my mission! If you don't feel good, go get lost in your work. You get homesick? Go to work. If you don't like how it's going, go to work!" Needless to say, I got the message. I went to work, and because of the effort and love I shared, it forever changed me as a man.

I share that message because he was a military man, and he played a massive role in my life. My baseball coaches, dad, and real estate mentors had the same style. I became a machine when it came to working and achieving. However, my emotions were blocked, and I didn't allow myself to feel sorry for myself. But really, all I was doing was blocking myself from processing vulnerabilities such as loneliness, frustration, or sadness. I had shit to do.

It wasn't until I started journeying inward that I learned there was more to life than being the best and taking first place. Around this time, I heard the quote that I've mentioned previously, "Success without fulfillment is the ultimate failure," which hit me right in the gut. I had stopped loving what I was doing. Sitting in the front row of an NBA basketball game wasn't even exciting, and frankly, I couldn't figure out why people cared so much about a stupid game. The parties and events I was throwing became routine, and I felt as if they were expected by the people around me instead of appreciated. I was successful by every measure, but missed true fulfillment in most every way.

Thankfully, I allowed this to lead me on a journey of self. Why did I always feel like I needed to prove myself to others? To prove that I was enough? To prove that I was loveable? Why did I think that if others saw me and knew everything about me, they wouldn't love me? I hid every part that I thought would make me look weak. I overposted on social media to show the world I was enough. God bless me, I was ignorant, but I was screaming for others to give me a sense of worthiness because of my achievements. Really, I was try-ing to say, "I promise I'm worthy of your love. Please love me."

A few years back, I read Lewis Howes's book *The Mask of Mas-culinity*, which taught me how to embrace vulnerability, shed my mask, and be seen for all of me, including the good, the bad, and the shameful. This pushed me to open up to a few of my closest friends. This was so scary because I genuinely didn't know if they would still love me once they knew I didn't have life completely figured out. What happened next was a miracle. They all loved me so much more. The best part was that **I could finally, for the first time, trust the love they were giving me.** They KNEW me and STILL loved me! As usually happens when you're vulnerable, they even opened up to me. The next thing I knew, I found myself appreciating them even more!

Friends whom I saw as the giants of the world, the most badass dudes in town, came clean and told me everything, from having wives who abused them to tragic moments as kids when someone had molested them. In these moments, I knew these guys would go from friends to brothers for life. We were all the same. We all had one issue or another.

I remember one of my best friends pulling a few of us aside one night and asking us if we could help him. He was about to be a dad and feeling the full pressure of stepping into that role. It's important to note, this friend looks like Brad Pitt, has a beautiful supermodel wife, and is a part-owner of a business with a seven-figure income. Yet, here he was, shedding his mask and asking us to remind him he was worthy of the role of a dad. Of all the people in the world I thought needed words of affirmation, he wasn't one of them. I laughed aloud; this man was everything a person should aspire to be, and he was being vulnerable and asking for support. I loved that man more than I ever had before. It allowed me to know I was a special person in his life, and that he, like every other man alive, needed brotherhood and friends to support him and build him up.

One of my favorite lines from *The Mask of Masculinity*, reads, "Stripped of the various masks of masculinity, we're free to be who we actually are. We can love. We can find purpose. We can connect." This is the new masculinity. This means you must have firm boundaries. You're not leaky with your finances or sexual energy. You are committed to your family, and you are 100% in integrity. You are strong both physically and mentally. But most importantly, you are strong enough to take off your mask and be seen, allowing those around you to see your weakness and to love you anyway. A man is brave enough to ask for help and willing to surrender into a loved one's arms and cry when needed.

One of the men in We Are The They had a beautiful experience after one of our in-person events. He was married with young children, and he did everything he could to provide for his family. We all looked up to him. But a few years prior, he had visited some strip clubs on a work trip and never told his wife about it. He came clean for the first time during a group cacao ceremony hosted by my friend Christine. It was a safe environment where he could freely share that he had been wearing this mask and had not been honest with himself, his family, or us. He committed to go home and tell his wife the next day.

True to his word, he told her. Terrified of what would happen, he did it anyway. He dared to get back into integrity. At first, she was sad and disappointed. Naturally, it took her a couple of hours to process it. He told me that after giving her space, she came to him and lovingly held him on the couch. She thanked him for telling her and for coming clean. She said that she still loved him and wanted to help him with any other issues he needed.

That night, when he called me, he told me through his tears, "Jimmy, I was pretty sure my wife loved me all these years. But tonight, she saw me for everything that I am, and now, for the first time in my marriage, I KNOW that she loves me." What a gift we give ourselves, those we love, and the world when we are vulnerable, authentic, and in integrity.

Another man in the group went home from one of our retreats and told his wife about a pornography problem he had since he was 12 years old. He'd never told a soul. Afterward, he told me that he hadn't been able to celebrate a day of his life because he always thought to himself, "If they knew who I really was, they wouldn't celebrate me." He was in his mid-thirties and never realized how loveable he was. He had the same experience with his wife as the other guy, and now he gets to live as a FREE man—to be seen and loved for who he is, who he isn't, and who he is becoming.

This is how you free your soul and heal the loneliness that men in the world suffer from. It is only through being open that we can heal our wounds. This allows the next generation of strong men to not only be strong in self-discipline, but also strong enough to let their emotions in and forgive themselves when they fall short. I am so grateful that I discovered this for myself in my mid-thirties, and it is the gift of my life to help other men like you, your significant others, and even teens learn these valuable lessons.

Be Connected

A few years back, I went on a safari in Botswana, Africa. It was an overnight journey, so we got to sleep in the middle of the bush, surrounded by animals. A honey badger walked right up to my leg, monkeys swung above our tents all night, and we could hear wild animals while we slept. The following day, we woke up and began the safari. Just five minutes in, we came across a pack of lions. They had been less than 300 yards from us all night long. As we sat and marveled at these creatures, I noticed one of the mama lions started to make her way over to the vehicle. I got a little nervous because it was an open-air vehicle, and the lioness clearly could have jumped in and attacked if it wanted to. I expressed my concern to the driver, and he responded, "This is why it is so important to stay in the vehicle. All the lions see us as one giant creature. The second you walk outside alone, the lions will see your weakness, and that's when they attack." And so it is in life.

There's an old saying, "If you want to go fast, go alone. If you want to go far, go together." I would add, "If you want to go fast and far, you need to go with a tribe!"

Connection is the antidote to toxicity. Staying suppressed or having volcanic explosions by not knowing how to express and release emotions is the cause of all toxic masculinity. Men who bottle up their emotions are angry, irritable, diseased, unhappy, and terminally unfulfilled. To live in a safer, freer world for everyone, of all backgrounds or orientation, we must honor what it truly is to be a man.

We Are The They is the No. 1 place for healthy masculinity because it allows men to be comfortable with themselves and get through any situation life throws at them. It's a place where being a man is celebrated—a place where you are celebrated—and gives you the opportunity to live the life you deserve.

I am glad you are here and glad you have made it this far . . . . Let's keep going.

7

Be *That* Friend

From HOPELESS to HEROIC

"You can have everything in life you want, if you will just help other people get what they want."

—Zig Ziglar

I HAVE INCREDIBLE friends. Seriously. I'm humbled, yet so grateful for the people I have in my life. I've been many less-than-favorable things in my life—a workaholic, a disinterested lover, an obsessive partner, an unhealthy eater—but one thing I've made sure of is that I'm there for my friends.

I can't emphasize enough just how important friendships are. They're one of the cornerstones to a beautiful life because whom you experience life with is what makes it amazing. If you have good friends around, you think more clearly, you make better decisions, you act better, and you have added meaning to your life. Authentic friendships are becoming less and less common, but they're worth the effort.

A few years ago, I was on a houseboat trip to Lake Powell with a bunch of friends. We were partying it up, having a great time, but then I felt something strange. We were supposed to stay till Sunday night, but I woke up Saturday morning and knew I had to leave. There was a friend several states away that needed me and it couldn't wait. He didn't call; I was called. Mind you, this was a friend who was struggling with his mental health. I shared his powerful thoughts on suicide in Chapter 2, but at the time, he wasn't on stable ground. He'd generally been on my mind, and had come up in conversations with mutual friends, but that morning in Lake Powell, he was all I could think about. The impression, intuition, God, or whatever you want to call it told me, "Jimmy, you need to go see him. Like right now. You need to leave this morning." I had someone take me back to the marina, drove six hours home, and took a flight out that night to get to him.

When I was on my way, I called and told him I was coming, saying I wanted to go hiking the next day. We had a long drive to get to the place we'd hike the next day and hung out casually in a hotel room that night. Nothing of significance happened. The next day, halfway through our hike, he cut through the silence, "Why are you here?"

"What are you talking about?" I asked.

He repeated himself, "Why are you here?"

"I don't know? I felt like I needed to come out. I just felt like I should."

He started crying and showed me his wrist, "I tried to kill myself two weeks ago, but the only reason I stopped is that I didn't want my daughter to find me in the shower. I've been hanging on for dear life every day since then."

I was stunned, "Brother, talk to me. What's this about?"

The full picture finally came out. His marriage was not working; it hadn't been for years, and for over nine months, they had very little romance and no sex. Growing up, he had a mom who wasn't very affectionate, and unfortunately, his wife wasn't either. He'd had limited feminine affection his entire life. Unexpectedly, he started getting attention from a woman at work and the attraction became mutual. While they didn't sleep together, they had an emotional affair. The woman's husband found out and told my buddy's wife. He knew he'd messed up, but the verbal abuse he received in return was over the top.

This guy had gone nine months without any intimacy, finally found a small spark of affection, and now he thought he was the worst human in the world. In his mind, he was the clear villain. In my mind, this guy was just trying to be loved. Here he was, one of the best fathers I'd ever seen, wanting to have an authentic, intimate relationship with his wife and was being shut out. I made it clear he was the hero of his story; at worst he wasn't the villain.

For years, he hadn't seen himself in any other light than the "bad guy." All it took was that one reframe, and his life changed forever. Even though there was a lot of tragedy in the entire situation, I just laughed with him. I told him, "You either have to ask for intimacy in your marriage, or you have to get out."

No one should go nine months without intimacy. It's fighting a losing battle. I promised him that if he put in the work, he'd see that his life could be more than he ever thought possible. It could be anything he wanted. Although he never fully overcame his depression, he improved significantly. To me, he is the world's greatest dad, but to the outside world, people wouldn't ever know. It's not like he's wearing a cape. Like most true heroes, nobody's writing articles in the paper about him. But he never misses one important date with his daughter. Even on days he doesn't have his daughter, they go hang out together.

A couple of years after the hike, we both went on a trip to Central America. He was newly single, but the nagging belief that he'd never find love again was keeping him locked in place. He still hadn't been with another woman. On a flight from Guatemala to Honduras, I spotted a stunning yoga instructor and told my friend, "You're sitting right there." Since it was one of the local airlines where you can sit anywhere, I made him sit next to her while I sat further back. They hit it off during the flight and ended up spending the entire night together.

The next day, when he came out of his room, he had tears streaming down his face. This strong guy, a former college baseball player, told us, "In my darkest days, when I felt hopeless, I never imagined my life could be this good." This was one of my proudest moments. I'd been there for him at his lowest, not with earth-shattering advice or all the right words, but with empathy and a view of his life that he couldn't see for himself. That's what being *that* friend looks like.

The Three Types of Friends

According to Aristotle, there are three types of friendships:

1. **Friendships of Utility:** These common friendships exist between you and someone who is useful to you in some way.
2. **Friendships of Pleasure:** These are between you and someone whose company you enjoy, making up the bulk of most friendships.
3. **Friendships of the Good:** Deeply rooted connections that are based on vulnerability, authenticity, and doing things together for each other's benefit and a greater good.

When people say someone's not a true friend, they're comparing a Friendship of Utility or Pleasure with someone they are unable to connect with on the deepest levels. They're wanting brotherhood, sisterhood, or freedom to just be themselves around family members, but instead, they remain at surface levels. For example, with friends of pleasure, you enjoy doing things together. But when the thing ends, so, too, does the friendship. At the third level of friendship, it's based on virtues, shared values, and morals. There's a certain level of goodness that you have to have to remain in that friendship.

It's essential to find the people who bring out the best in you to grow and inspire friendship. Friendships of Utility or Pleasure are very real, beneficial, and supportive. But to give and receive the best aspects of what friendship can be, you need to aim for the highest and deepest form of friendship, which is one based on virtue and shared goodness.

Sadly, most people don't believe they have the skills, tools, network, and resources to start, grow, and maintain good friendships. Loneliness is an epidemic. It's a multifaceted issue involving complex personal psychology, sociology, and someone's inability to feel connected to people in a genuine way. Putting it more plainly, loneliness is feeling like there's a gap between the relationships you want and the ones you actually have. Even if you're not alone, you might feel lonely if your connections with others aren't satisfying. If this feeling persists, it will make you unhappy and is likely to make you sick.

While loneliness itself doesn't directly kill people, it contributes to a variety of health problems that lead to premature death. Studies have shown that loneliness can be as harmful as smoking 15 cigarettes a day and can increase the risk of premature death by 45%! Furthermore, loneliness and social isolation often lead to conditions like depression, heart disease, and dementia. A study published in the *Heart* journal in 2016 found that loneliness and social isolation increased the risk of having a heart attack or stroke by nearly 30%.

After the tragic social distancing mandates as a result of the global pandemic in 2020, the subject of loneliness is gaining attention. Awareness of a problem is the first step in resolving it. I pray that people are actively doing things to reduce isolation and hopelessness, and embracing being the hero of their own life. There are millions of people worldwide who are in need of deep, loving, and authentic friendships. Here are some sobering statistics that put this epidemic in perspective:

- A survey by Cigna in 2020 suggested that about 61% of Americans reported feeling lonely, up from 54% in 2018.
- According to the Office for National Statistics in the United Kingdom, between April 2020 and February 2021, 5% of people in Great Britain (2.6 million adults) reported "always" feeling lonely.
- A survey in 2019 by the Australian Red Cross found that one in four Australians are lonely almost all of the time or on a regular basis. One in four! So sad.

- The elderly are particularly at risk, with a 2020 report from the National Academies of Sciences, Engineering, and Medicine indicating that more than one-third of adults aged 45 and older feel lonely, and nearly one-fourth of adults aged 65 and older are considered to be socially isolated in the United States.

It's critical to address loneliness in ourselves and those around use. While there's nothing wrong with being alone, and I think it's essential for most people (especially people like me), staying there for long periods of time is a dark place. True friendship is the antidote. In the following sections, I'll share what I've learned about creating authentic, lasting friendships. To help me with this chapter, I reached out to my closest friends, asking them for their input. What they shared didn't surprise me, but it fed my soul, and once again, made me deeply grateful for them.

Do Your Friends Let You Unapologetically Be Yourself?

A good friend always sees the good in you and doesn't try to change you. But that doesn't mean they'll give you a pass to be hurtful, rude, obnoxious, or entitled. If you're acting out, a friend has the love for you to call you into a better version of yourself. They don't try to change you, they see the good in you, always. I love what Bernard Meltzer said on this: "A true friend is someone who thinks that you are a good egg even though he knows that you are slightly cracked."

A true friendship is not being worried about judgment or loss of friendship when you make a misstep. A friend knows your heart. They know who you are. They trust you, are quick to give grace for mistakes, and they seek to first understand you.

True friendship also comes with boundaries. If a friend has done something hurtful and they haven't sought out reconciliation because of their pride, you have no obligation to keep them around. Setting clear boundaries may feel like you're hurting them and creating distance, but the prideful party is the one that's pushing the friendship further away. A good friend provides a space where you're safe to be yourself, and also faces disagreements head-on.

Friends who heal together, stay together. This is how you access a Friendship of the Good where you don't have to be anything other than who you are. You're safe to share your wins, but also your struggles. While you feel safe to be vulnerable, a good friend is always calling you up into the best version of yourself, not accepting your BS, and lovingly reminding you to be accountable to your true, highest self.

Do Your Friends Hold You to a Higher Standard?

While a friend shouldn't be hypercritical, if you've done something hurtful, they should feel compelled to call you on it. You'd apologize, and then, that would be the end of it. I've been blessed to receive this from my closest friends. Even though I don't hear their inner dialogue, it probably sounded something like this: "I know Jimmy, and I know that he's not a bad person. He wasn't trying to be hurtful with what he just said, but I need to let him know that wasn't in his or my best interest." Situations that could drive people further apart are the same opportunities to bring people closer together, but this requires vulnerability, authenticity, and integrity.

Several years ago, a group of my high school friends and I went to Alaska. During our trip, one friend made an inappropriate joke. Without hesitation, we all stepped in saying, "Come on, that's not okay. We don't speak that way. What are you even talking about?" We didn't think less of him, nor did he become less of a friend to us. There was no judgment, but there was an immediate correction. We just guided him toward having better thoughts and ideas. That's what true friends do. They let you see your blind spots that you can't see on your own.

At a recent birthday party, my friends and I were sitting around a fire and one of my closest friends asked me, "Jimmy, if we were to trade places for a day and you could be me, what's the first thing you would do?" Without hesitation I said, "Steve, you need better friends. You give your time and attention to people who don't deserve it. They're not a good influence on you, and it keeps some people from getting closer to you because we don't want to be around them." A few days later, he told me that was one of the most impactful things he'd ever heard because he knew it was true. He was so grateful that I had unapologetically given him that information.

A genuine friend doesn't hesitate to call you out when you're faltering. I recall one moment in particular when my friend Cameron decided to say something to our buddy who was bordering on alcoholism. Cameron privately confronted him, teary-eyed, telling him, "Hey, man, real talk. I don't think you understand how big of an issue this is in your life. I'm worried about you, and we need to do something." His sincerity moved our friend, who immediately quit drinking, lost 40 pounds, and now, rarely drinks.

One of the greatest actions you can take as a friend is maintaining an extremely high standard of your relationships. Everyone should be aware that you will not tolerate anyone in your life if they could be detrimental to your other friends. As a result, your friends trust your judgment in people, knowing that you'd never associate with anyone harmful. If someone proves otherwise and they won't change their ways, your friends know you will immediately distance them, for your own good and for the good of those you love.

Do Your Friends Win When You Win?

Pay attention to how people react when you are celebrating. You can really tell if someone is a good friend if they're genuinely excited for you. Not everyone says things on the nose like, "That's amazing!

I'm so happy for you!" But when you hear things like, "That surprises me," or "I wouldn't expect that. Good job," those little things are a big deal. There's no need to judge how effective someone is at congratulating you. It's your job to feel their heart and be grateful that they really are happy for you, no matter how they convey it.

Don't hold back, and make it clear to your friends that you're absolutely thrilled for them when they're celebrating. Most people feel shame around being super expressive, especially men, but I promise you, everyone deserves praise. Even if someone gives you the humble pie spiel and tries to shut it down, they deserve it. Lots of people feel like the guy who said, "If people really knew me, they wouldn't celebrate me." If someone is triggered or brushes off praise, they are the ones who likely need it the most.

Giving a friend the gift of another great friend is one of the most valuable things you can offer. One of the things I enjoy the most is introducing my friends to each other. If I find out a couple of guys I introduced went golfing without me, I don't think, "What the hell? Why didn't they invite me?" I feel gratitude. Even though I wasn't able or invited to join them, my friendship with each of them facilitated that moment. By connecting friends, you enhance your own friendships exponentially. Some people hesitate to introduce their friends to each other, or they feel left out if they aren't invited to every gathering. But as a true friend, it's not about being included in every event. It's about the happiness you feel for those friends and the satisfaction you get from making the connection.

Do Your Friends Ask How You're Doing or What You're Doing?

I love to call my closest friends just because I have something funny to share. I have nothing of real importance, and it usually begins with, "You're not going to believe what happened to me today." The conversation is like a *Seinfeld* episode. It has nothing to do with anything, and we just laugh our asses off because we truly see and appreciate each other. It's often completely ridiculous, but it's funny to us. I didn't call to "get" anything, I called to connect. Those moments are the moments that separate utility from connection.

I call five people every day because, most of the time, people only call their "friends" when they need something or on special occasions. True friendship is when you call for no reason other than to just talk and see how they are. I recommend you do this as an exercise. Here are the two rules: Don't ask for anything. Don't offer anything. Just call and chitchat. The people I'm the closest to in the world are these people. We talk about anything and nothing.

In true friendship, there's no room for neediness. You just exist in each other's lives, secure in the knowledge that you're available for one another. Therefore, when you really do need something, asking for it isn't awkward. It's about vulnerability, simply saying, "Hey, could you help me with this?" or "What's your take on this?" There's no neediness, or feelings of, "We should hang out more." You understand they're busy, and you're comfortable extending invitations. If they can't make it, that's okay because you know they would if they could.

Another sign of a healthy friendship is the ability to bypass superficial "catching up." With my closest friends, I could call them right now, and we'd pick up the conversation as if we've been talking every day. We may not have spoken for two months, but we don't need to speak about all the things that happened in the time in between, make excuses, or apologize. We just dive into the meat of the conversation. If I need something, I can ask without a preamble.

The reason I make those five calls is because it's uncommon for people to reach out themselves. Often, we hear people say, "If you're depressed or having a hard time, call me," but those struggling aren't going to. I've had numerous individuals ask me, "Jimmy, how did you know to call? How did you know it was just the right time?"

Many times, I had a gut feeling to call them. More often than not, they were simply on the list of calls for that day. But because I consistently make those calls, I inevitably connect with people who need a conversation. True friends reciprocate this care, checking on how I'm feeling as often as I check on them. They know to ask more about *how* I'm doing, rather than just seeing *what* I'm doing.

Are Your Friends Present?

A good friend is there even if it's been a week, a month, or over a year and I need their help. They ask me for help. They let me serve them as much as they serve me. A good friend shares an energetic flow that lifts us both. While it's critical to have people whom you can go to in hard times, it's less about "What have you done for me lately?" than it is, "What have we done lately to make the world a little better?"

You know someone is your person when presence is all that you need. The ability to just share time with each other, no need to fill up the space with words, deeds, or noise is where real intimacy in a friendship comes from. If you struggle to be fully present with someone, it's never going to be able to become a Friendship of the Good because the need to do things will make it one of utility or pleasure.

It's impossible to be genuinely connected to someone if every time you're together, you talk about other people or other things. Bringing other people or things into a conversation serves as a way to create a false sense of connection, but true intimacy is speaking to each other about each other. People create pseudo-connection all the time. They find things to agree or disagree on, serving as a superficial way to "know" each other. But connecting in a deep and profound way requires an openness to really being seen, being heard, not fearing being disagreed with, and not looking for the other person to validate you. Again, this is where vulnerability and authenticity serve as the bedrock of long-lasting friendships.

Are Your Friends Loyal?

A true friend has my back, whether I'm in the room or not. They'll stand up against naysayers and critics, not because I'm infallible, but because they understand my intentions and trust I understand theirs. Have you ever considered how your friends speak about you when you're not around? Are they saying things that might cast you in a negative light? A true friend wouldn't. You'd likely only discover how they talk about you in your absence through another loyal friend who speaks up for you and shares what's been said. While this could be seen as perpetuating gossip, you have an obligation to your friends to be loyal.

Someone once questioned me about one of my friends, saying, "I really don't like this guy. Here's why." The person who was questioning this individual was the leader of the group I was around, and with a crowd present, I felt pressured. Still, I told them why I valued him as a friend. I shared some lesser-known qualities and experiences that built credibility for him. I said, "There's a lot of hearsay about him, but I've never personally seen a reason not to be his friend. So, unless proven otherwise, I must tell you, he's my friend, and I have his back." Even the critic appreciated my defense of this person, and hopefully, he learned a valuable lesson in not being a shit-talker.

Being a loyal friend means confronting difficult situations, not helping to hide them. Many people equate loyalty with covering up wrongdoings, but doing so is the most disloyal thing you can do. I've seen friends not be upfront with other friends, which just hurts them in the long run. Being loyal to someone who's dishonest or exploiting others isn't real loyalty. In fact, it's clear disloyalty to those who are affected.

A best friend is loyal to what's best for them, not loyal to their bullshit. When one of my best friends went to a strip club and wanted us to help him hide it from his family, we became protectors of his family since we were his best friends. People think loyalty is, "Oh, I can't tell your wife," or, "I can't call you out on this. I have to just love you and support you." But that's not what a best friend does. A best friend says, "How do you want to handle this before we talk to your wife? I'm going to be there every step of the way. We'll watch your kids and help you with whatever you need. But, brother, we're going to get this fixed." These moments are terrifying, but it's not quite as scary when you have a friend that walks with you through the darkness.

Be Heroic

When I was in my twenties, I had a lot of friends who tried to make me look stupid or look bad in front of a girl. One time, I had a girl whom I was super interested in tell me she was running 15 minutes late to meet up. I sat on the back porch reading, waiting for her to arrive. When I finally went into the front room, one of my roommates was hitting on her. They were cuddled on the couch about to head beyond that. Needless to say, the relationship with her was over and so was any chance at a deep friendship with my roommate.

As friends, sometimes it's hard enough when we're working with each other. It's next to impossible if we're working against each other. At that moment, I made it a point that I would never have people in my life who don't respect me or don't respect themselves.

In stark contrast to my life in my twenties, I honestly believe I have some of the best friends in the world. We Are The They is filled with guys I've known for years, and many more I've only known for a few months, but it feels like I've known them forever. These men, their wives, and their children all have friends they can trust because they're meeting each other from a place of, you guessed it, vulnerability, authenticity, and integrity.

Brotherhood isn't bought, it's earned, worked for, and cultivated. It takes true courage, commitment, and compassion to be a friend.

Over the years, I've become close friends with Erwin McManus, one of the top speakers in the country. He runs the Mosaic Church in Los Angeles, and his book *The Genius of Jesus* is one of my favorite books. When I was doing my annual event in Utah, I needed a keynote speaker. I called him up and asked. He said he'd love to! He loved what I had created with We Are The They, and he saw the mission I'm on to bring people together in a really big way. This was great and all, but I still had to ask the million-dollar question: "How much do you cost?" He said, "Jimmy, I'll do it under one condition. You have to go to dinner with me the night before. Spend some time with me. I just want to get to know you better." Immediately, I knew that this was my guy. From that point on, he and I became close friends. Why? Because we both knew we had servant-hearts.

Having a servant-heart and finding others who have the same is your best way to find and keep extraordinary friendships. This is what it means to build Friendships of the Good. With all of the problems our world faces, including our individual struggles, having a true friend makes the journey through toxicity into triumph that much sweeter. I cannot imagine where I'd be today without the friends who have filled my life with purpose and joy.

A friend is someone who is there when you need them and still checks up on you when you don't. A good friend is an honest mirror. They beam back your highlights, and they don't let you hide from your darkness. A friend expects maintenance, but isn't high maintenance. They want you to win and won't let you sit around and be less than you could. A good friend is made, not found.

Jim Rohn says, "Friends are those beautiful people who know everything about you, and still like you." That couldn't be more true. A friend likes you for you, encourages you to be your best self, and accepts you when you fail, oftentimes in ways that even family can't. That's why friends are the family you choose. They're the ones you laugh the hardest with and create the best memories with.

A best friend will drop everything and fly, drive, or run to you in your times of need or celebration.

Good friendships can be gained instantly and held for a lifetime, and you spend time together whenever possible because they always leave you better than they found you.

That's what it looks like to be *that* friend.

If you think you don't get enough of *that* kind of friendship, start by giving it.

Start right now.

Call five people and remember the two rules: Don't ask for anything. Don't offer anything. Just call and see how they're doing. And when it's time to end the conversation, do so quickly. No neediness, no awkwardness, no explaining, no apologizing—just being *that* friend, for their sake and yours too.

8

Be Love to Get Loved

From SELFISH to SATISFIED

"Being deeply loved by someone gives you strength, while loving someone deeply gives you courage."

—Lao Tzu

EVERYTHING ABOUT BEING an extraordinary friend applies to being in a romantic relationship. The only difference is the kind of intimacy you share with your partner. Intimacy can be uncomfortable and confronting at first, but it's the only way to have genuine connections. The catch is ensuring your romantic partner isn't the only person you can be vulnerable with. It's not sustainable to be reliant on a single person to feel safe, connected, and loved.

Having great friends, aka a supportive community, is the solid foundation needed to build romantic relationships. The days of being a lone wolf are over. That may have been badass in 2010, but we're in an entirely new era. There are too many things at stake, individually and collectively, to try and figure things out on our own. To allow romantic relationships to flourish, you first have to master your friendships. If your friendships already support your emotional, intellectual, and spiritual needs, your romantic relationships can evolve unburdened by need. A healthy romantic relationship will add to your abundance, not be working to fill a hole.

If you're in a romantic relationship and have just begun learning how to be a great friend, you don't have to break up with them and start over. You can start in whichever romantic situation you find yourself in right now. So, before doing anything impulsive, keep reading to discover what constitutes a healthy, satisfying relationship.

Free to Simply Be

One night, my buddies and their wives were hanging out at my house. Looking around, one guy realized that, in the past, he couldn't trust his friends around his wife when he was gone. He knew that if they got a chance, they would try something with her. He said, "Jimmy, I know if I couldn't be here tonight, but she was, I would sleep with absolutely no fear of something inappropriate happening toward her. I have so much trust and faith in these friendships that it wouldn't even cross my mind because of who you guys are." That level of respect among your friends and your significant other means everything. It's the only kind of friendship or relationship I'll have.

If a loved one told you they had accidentally killed somebody, if you really loved them, you would not shame, judge, or reject them. You'd say, "I'm so sorry. You must feel terrible, and that's okay. We'll get through this together." To really show up for them, your immediate response would be one of understanding, providing a safe place to have any conversation. Having an impulse to protect, support, and understand those you love is nonnegotiable in a relationship. This is what is commonly called "holding space," and we'll dive deeper into this essential practice in this chapter.

If your romantic partner isn't the person you feel the safest with, you'll be constantly hurt and let down. Either seek professional help to heal together, or if they're unwilling to put in the work, you must leave the relationship. If you can't completely be yourself with 100% vulnerability, then the relationship is pointless. The best time to end a toxic relationship is immediately. Drawing it out just makes things increasingly complicated.

Having the freedom to express yourself and trust that your partner won't reject you is a basic requirement. That said, if you're expressing something hurtful that's directed at them, they have no obligation to just take it. That's an abuse of their love for you. Yet, if you're saying something judgmental, ignorant, or unconscious, a good partner would simply say, "What are you even talking about?" They wouldn't try to change their mind, and if they're in touch with themself, they won't take what you're saying personally.

These situations are often volatile because most people who are wrong in what they're saying tend to be combative or defensive.

It's in no way the role of a significant other to tolerate these behaviors. However, one of life's greatest gifts is to be loved by someone who hears you say something that's completely off base and loves you anyways. Someone can love you through a variety of tactics, like asking one of the best questions anyone can offer, which is, "What do you mean by that?" Or, if it's not something worth exploring, you both can laugh, and hopefully have the humility and self-awareness to not be hard on each other for making a mistake.

The goal is to have a relationship that's completely vulnerable and open with each other. Through that, each partner is going to feel completely loved and respected. Regardless of what is said or done, both parties will never disrespect or treat each other like less. You will never talk down to them, embarrass them, or make them feel small.

I have this same rule with my friends. I will never spend time with people who would belittle me or make me feel small in any way, shape, or form. That's what we did as kids. I know now that my person and my friends really know me. Since I've been willing to be vulnerable and have shown them my heart, they've got my back.

What Every Man Wants

A few years back, I was attending a conference with a close friend. He had good relationships with his kids, his work was great, everything was in order financially, and he had amazing friends. Yet, he was struggling with his marriage. They'd been fighting constantly since I met him, and they'd both cheated on each other. It was a mess of a relationship.

In contrast, the speaker on the stage was a mutual friend of ours who had built a fortune in real estate and was now a well-known public speaker. I'd heard him give this speech a few times, so I was moderately invested but not completely paying attention. But do you know who was all in? His wife was in the front row. She was grinning from ear to ear with the biggest smile I've ever seen. She was giddy as a schoolgirl watching her husband speak.

They had been married for over 40 years, yet here she was, filming him, taking pictures of him, and being his biggest fan. She'd probably heard him give that speech a hundred times, yet she could not have been more happy nor more proud of her husband.

My friend said, "Jimmy, I would trade every dollar I've ever made and every accomplishment I've ever had for my wife to look at me just one time the way his wife looks at him." He went on, "If I could only give you one piece of marital advice, it's this: Find a woman who adores you."

For most men, being in a relationship with someone who adores, respects, and is proud to be with him—that's everything. But this level of love must be earned, not handed out. As men, it's our sacred responsibility to be the kind of man that a person can't help but be proud of. By being completely in integrity, you'll be attractive to many people, but your significant other will know you choose them, every single time. Having a partner that truly supports you and your goals means they'll call you into integrity if you're not in alignment. Every guy knows when his partner adores him, and his partner knows when he's fully committed to them. If the two of them do that, there's nothing they won't do for each other. That's a power couple. The alternative is a toxic time-bomb.

It Was Me All Along

Almost everyone has had their heart broken, been cheated on, or treated badly at some point in their lives. We come into relationships with scars and bruises. Many people use relationships to deal with those scars, but this is a recipe for disaster. While it's common to feel like someone can "complete you," if people enter into a relationship from a perceived deficit, the relationship becomes a way to feel better rather than a place of mutual respect, honor, and selfless-ness. Do the work first to avoid those toxic behaviors.

Codependency, while not a formally recognized personality dis-order, is a behavioral condition in a relationship where one person, or both parties, enables another person's poor mental health, imma-turity, irresponsibility, or under-achievement. This, along with out-right narcissism or other kinds of relational abuse, is a product of selfish, toxic dynamics. People inherit these behaviors from unhealed ancestral patterns that come from parents, culture, and society. Without good examples of how to engage in beautiful, supportive, and intimate relationships, people will often get into bad relation-ships that reflect their childhoods.

While it's true that opposites attract, like also attracts like. Someone who's a victim of childhood abuse is statistically the most likely person to become an abuser. This is often done in self-defense so as to not be continually hurt. More often, they will get into a romantic relationship where they continue to be abused and experi-ence life as a victim. It's a grim topic, but we can't ignore it. Various studies have estimated that roughly 1 in 3 women and 1 in 4 men have experienced some form of physical violence by an intimate partner. Nearly half of all women and men in the United States will experience psychological aggression in their lifetimes.

These figures are estimated from those who reported abuse, with the true figures likely higher due to the hidden and private nature of abusive relationships. These estimates also don't factor in the nor-malization of abusive behaviors in certain cultures. There are many people being abused who might not even know to call it that. This breaks my heart to write about.

As I noted in Chapter 6, the purpose of my life is to share my tremendous love for all of God's children. I'm not speaking about this from the outside. I've been hurt many times, and I've hurt some peo-ple I was intimate with because I didn't know how to hold space.

Holding space is offering a judgment-free zone, and it's so much more than words. Truly holding space is all about your body language, the energy in the room, and it's a place where someone can truly be seen. It's less about anything you have to say, and simply allowing someone to share whatever comes up for them, free of judgment.

I've done this horribly, which is one of the reasons I never had a healthy relationship while I was in the church. I had so much judgment around people's actions. I was in constant search of "the one," but unsurprisingly, no one was ever good enough. It wasn't until I left the church that I quit caring *what* they were doing, and cared much more about *how* they were doing. Once I realized that I didn't need to uphold a delusional ideal of perfection and project that on those whom I loved, we were free to love each other, as we were. I stopped searching for "the one" when I realized whom I needed wasn't someone else who made everything in my life better—it was me all along.

I spent years exploring what self-love is, and what it's not. It's not spa days, candles, fuzzy socks, and binge-watching Netflix. Self-love is getting into the damn ice bath at 7:30 a.m. It's eating a grapefruit when I want a cheeseburger. It's not dissociating when someone tells you that you hurt them. It's being willing to be okay with not being okay all the time, and not reaching for something to make yourself feel better.

It's taken years of effort, accountability, and sacrifice to find satisfaction within myself. Then, and only then, have I truly been able to embrace the satisfaction that relationships offer me. Like the guy in my group who couldn't accept others' love because if people "really knew him," they wouldn't love him. Once that story ended and he got in touch with reality, he found love for himself and could trust the love he got from others. He realized that it was him all along, too.

At the time of writing this book, I'm not in a long-term relationship, but I can sense one is on the horizon. For years, I knew I wasn't being the best man I could be for myself. "The one" wasn't ready to join me because she's not going to settle for a version of me that is so much less than who I can be. Now that I've given myself the time and space I needed to love and accept myself, I'm ready to join my queen.

Treasure Is Found in the Depths

The goal of relationships isn't perfection, it's knowing that the beauty of life is in the mess. For example, it's not wrong to fight, only if you've learned to fight fair. According to Dr. John Gottman, "Conflict is growth trying to happen." Gottman's research has shown that couples that approach disagreements with mutual respect and openness to understanding each other's perspective tend to have stronger relationships. Fighting, in the context of a healthy relationship, does not include any harmful or abusive behaviors, but rather having disagreements or differing opinions. Instead of conflict leading to meltdowns, blowouts, and breakups, these moments are golden opportunities to improve communication, understand each other's perspectives, and grow as a couple.

Here are three rules to remember when "fighting" with your beloved:

1. Always remember you're talking to someone you love and care about.
2. Telling the truth and the facts of the situation both matter, but do so keeping the first rule in mind.
3. You're not in competition with each other. It's not about "winning" or being right. It's about exploring each other's edges and loving what you find.

The treasure of relationships can only be found after you've learned to love the imperfections. It's knowing the jewels are in the little things, the subtle moments. Like Robin Williams's iconic character in *Good Will Hunting* says, "You're not perfect, sport, and let me save you the suspense: this girl you've met, she's not perfect either. But the question is whether or not you're perfect for each other. That's the whole deal. That's what intimacy is all about."

When both of you are committed to growth and progress, even the messiest parts are beautiful. By letting go of preconceived ideas of what the relationship should look like, you allow the love itself to be perfect. The direction of the relationship becomes free to evolve and grow. That's where safety with each other enters because you both have permission to be less than perfect and make mistakes. This is true for a friendship, romantic relationship, or with yourself. I have very high expectations for myself, as I do for a partner. But I also give myself a lot of grace because I know myself and trust my heart.

Men don't want their motives or their heart being questioned. Simultaneously, no real man is mad when he makes a mistake, and his partner says, "Well, we're not doing that again." If his partner trusts his heart, they won't attack him personally or try to diminish his soul. Instead, they'll say, "Oh, we can do better than this," or "Honey, we don't talk to each other that way because we love each other." An honest, authentic relationship where both parties can nudge each other into integrity in a loving, nonjudgmental way is a hallmark of a union bound for success and deep satisfaction.

The River and the Riverbank

When presence in a friendship or attraction in a romantic relationship begins to fade, then the intimacy decreases. But, when two people are connected to each other, it's very easy to overlook any issues. If it's a toxic connection, then the appeal will come with highs and lows, creating a slamming together and then an intense push away. People can get addicted to trauma-bonded relationships or relationships of convenience, but as time goes on, attraction fades. When it does, partners will start to get upset and frustrated quickly. This doesn't necessarily mean it's a toxic relationship, but remember, conflict is an opportunity for growth.

Why does attraction fade? Surprisingly, it is not a physical issue. A bad diet, overwhelm, being medicated, alcohol, and a host of other lifestyle choices can lead to a decrease in the quality of a romantic connection. However, when someone loses attraction, it's often caused because of depolarization. Depolarization happens when two partners no longer have the interplay of masculine or feminine roles between them; for example, a partner who feels too stressed to relax into their feminine, or a partner who's too insecure to keep their masculine stronghold. Many people spend years of their life stuck in this cycle and get used to the loss of attraction. Thankfully, with the right actions, attraction can come back in an instant.

Masculine and feminine energies and their qualities are not gender-based. Every person has both within each of us, and we can embody either energy. Whatever energy is most dominant for you is what defines who you are. What's most important is knowing what your true nature is, embodying it, and being in integrity as you express yourself. I love what Matthew Fox said about this: "When the sacred masculine is combined with the sacred feminine inside each of us, we create the 'sacred marriage' of compassion and passion within ourselves." By doing this, we have access to our full self and our full range of expression.

While we have both within us, polarity is the key to a passionate and intimate relationship. *Polarity* is the term used for physical chemistry, the magnetic pull and the overwhelming physical response we feel when we meet someone with an energy attractive to our own. Think in terms of a battery—you cannot get a charge without both a strong positive and negative current. We need both to get a spark. Therefore, the more polarized those energies are, the stronger the attraction will be in the relationship. *Please note:* for the sake of simplicity, I'll be using traditional pronouns of he/him for masculine energy and she/her for feminine energy.

A feminine person can go from uptight and controlling to free and blossoming when her masculine partner makes her feel loved and appreciated. A masculine person can quickly get into his core essence with prayer, meditation, or contemplation. People think to be masculine, it's about lifting heavy weights or *doing* something, but it's to show up in a strong, confident way that only comes by being in touch with himself. Feminine energy tends to express itself through movement, while masculine energy comes home to itself through stillness. Sexual attraction, spiritual ecstasy, and intimate connection thrive in a relationship when there is a distinct polarity between energies of the individuals involved.

To be strong in your masculine energy, it takes work to be at a place in life where you don't need your life to be any one particular way. Believe me, my life has not become what I thought it was going to be. If I were directing things, and I had a chance to guide it wherever I wanted it to go, it would be entirely different than what it is today. To be blunt, I would have screwed up the whole thing. It wouldn't be nearly as beautiful, rich, and interesting, nor half as fun if I had tried to control it.

We tend to want things to be "perfect" and to go the way we plan. We don't love surprises, per se, but damn, they sure make life interesting! I hope that when anyone looks back on their life, they choose to see the divine orchestration of it all, regardless how tragic, chaotic, or insufficient it is in their own eyes. Nothing of value can be created in the present if there are any resentments from the past or fears of failure in the future. It's a characteristic of a healthy human to learn from all things, and this is why you need to retreat into prayer or meditation in the midst of the thunderstorm. Then, get your ass up and dance in the rain with your lover instead of wishing things weren't so stormy.

That's the beautiful potential of a relationship—when things don't go as planned, whether for the man or the woman, they're there for each other. Yet hardships can be depolarizing, and it can take work to bring back passion after moments, or seasons of difficulty. Fundamentally, to restore polarity, the masculine person allows the feminine person to be whatever she wants to be. He creates the frame in which she can dance, cry, vent, play, make a mess, and be who she is. He holds the space, knowing it's the safety she needs *and* the way to access the respect and adoration he craves. But, as he holds the frame, if he doesn't like how she's dancing, it doesn't matter because it's her dance and a man lives to let her dance.

For the feminine person, it's important that when she finds a partner, she is able to be her unfiltered, truest self. If people get together and hope the other is going to change, the relationship is going to be toxic from day one. For everyone, the goal should be to find somebody who knows themselves, knows what they want, takes action to get it (masculine energy), and is able to receive (feminine energy). The ultimate desire for a feminine person is having a masculine person who holds space without telling her how to dance. From that, she feels the safety to pour out all of her love for her man, and he feels the freedom to do anything required to maintain her outpouring of affection.

Masculine and feminine energies are like a river and the riverbank. Feminine energy needs the riverbank to be in its flow because if the riverbank is not there, the water is stagnant and lifeless. It's the frame that holds the canvas of art. It's the floor that supports the dancer. It's the stage that holds up the actor playing out the dramas of life. It's the riverbank that lovingly caresses the moving, living water.

However, if the masculine energy becomes too controlling, he'll constrict and narrow the riverbanks. This causes things to move too fast, more like a straight line, and that's usually not what she wants. He wants the freedom to guide her, and she wants the safety to trust where she's flowing. She also needs to push up against him and know he's sturdy, but if she needs more space, the riverbank moves with her. He's not rigid. He's not prideful. He's not controlling. True lasting romance is a dance between water and earth—river and riverbank—feminine and masculine.

Being One Isn't About Conforming

Many think that feminism is about women being the same as men. However, true feminism is understanding that women should have the same opportunities and be given the same respect as men. While topics like feminism and aspects of the LGBTQ+ community can be highly controversial, this is what I know: masculine and feminine energy is on a spectrum. Therefore, identity can be dynamic. The conditions that lend someone to being attracted to those of the same, opposite, or undefined identity is nearly impossible to succinctly discuss, but must be done with curiosity and respect.

Regardless of identity, we are all human, and we have the same relationship struggles, needs, and desires. This can be a complex and sensitive subject, yet through many conversations with my gay, lesbian, trans, and straight friends, I've found clarity at a time when it's greatly needed.

Every human being has an internal world and an external world. These worlds are intertwined and greatly influence each other. Your emotions and state of mind will manifest certain external real-life situations. Simultaneously, if you're in a certain setting or environment, it will likely influence your emotions, depending on its positive or negative vibe. While these worlds are not the same, they go hand in hand. Your masculine and feminine energies are a part of your inner world, and the level of awareness you have of them will determine your external reality via your likes, dislikes, experiences, and the kinds of relationships you attract.

Culturally, there's been an increase in awareness of the fact that everyone has both of these energies within, leading to a historic increase in diverse gender identities and unconventional relationship structures. This realization has led many people to change how they dress, express, and identify themselves. People who would have spent their lives ashamed to be who they are can now make sense of reality and find their place in the world. While many still suffer from hiding their identity, millions more don't feel alone for what they feel.

Identity and labels are not without their pitfalls. If someone feels an internal deficiency or insecurity and uses a label (asexual, bisexual, etc.) as a sense of control, it will not solve the underlying problem. Labels, like anything else used for selfish gain, is a short-term solution for a problem in the depths of someone's soul. I'm not recommending we get rid of labels. They are a necessary step in the process of self-realization, but if depended on, things stay superficial.

Someone who intellectually understands the fact they have both masculine and feminine energies within them is inherently more self-aware than someone who does not. Yet, if someone who "knows" claims an identity of gay, bisexual, or straight, but doesn't do the work to harmonize those energies internally, they're going to suffer.

A close friend, who is like a sister to me, told me that she was asexual. I knew some of her background, but was surprised by this revelation. I remained curious and wanted to understand why she chose this identity. At the time, she felt no sexual impulse whatsoever, therefore she identified as such. Knowing we had the safety to speak candidly, I later asked her if she felt a need to claim the identity of asexual as a safety net so she wouldn't have to explore why she wasn't interested in pleasing herself or being with a partner. Since I knew her well, I could see she was using the culturally accepted identity of asexual to justify a lack of desire to really feel and heal what was behind that choice. She appreciated the perspective as she starts the work that's been avoided.

It's become more common for someone who is heterosexual, and often in a conventional relationship, to identify as queer. While I firmly believe that everyone is entitled to feel however they feel, is that queer person really queer? Was my friend really asexual? For millions of people, yes, they are. For millions more, no, they're not. They're claiming something that's been culturally promoted as being more inclusive, virtuous, or to be accepted in their communities.

This is highly ironic because what was common in previous generations is that people who truly were gay, lesbian, and so on claimed the identity of being straight out of fear of being rejected for desiring to be with someone of the same sex. Regardless of the identity that's being claimed, if someone claims identity from a place of compensation, need for safety, or lusting for validation, it's not authentic. It lacks integrity, and it's selfish.

Another example of claiming something, but with huge consequences, are trans women (biological males) who compete and dominate in women's sports. By claiming this identity, but having clear biological advantages, it steals from the women who prepared their whole lives for those competitions. That's not equality of sexes, and it's fundamentally destructive to our society.

Claiming things from an unconscious place also happens in heterosexual, "conventional" relationships all the time, and it's a huge issue. A man who "claims" his wife, but is not safe or loving to her, is a highly toxic man. A woman in her feminine polarity wants to be claimed by her man if, and only if, she can 100% trust him to not abuse her or take advantage of her trust. The problem is that most people haven't seen healthy examples of romantic relationships. Therefore, most people haven't entered into, as Matthew Fox said, a "sacred marriage of compassion and passion" within themselves, leading hurt people to end up hurting other people within all backgrounds, orientations, and identities.

Then how do we explore and find out who we truly are before we adopt a label or get into a relationship?

Do you know who you are, really?

Does the thought of committing to just one woman sound stupid?

Are you afraid of trusting a man to be in his masculine polarity?

Are you really okay with not having sex, or have you had a hurtful experience that's making you not want to be vulnerable or open your heart?

Any kind of romantic relationship will not be satisfying on a soul level until the truth about masculine and feminine polarity has been grasped in an internal way. This means the knowledge must integrate and turn into embodied wisdom. It's the humble confidence that can be seen from a distance. When you see someone who has it, it's clear they know who they are.

This is what it means to "be one" with yourself. It doesn't mean forcing yourself to be okay with any and everything, and it definitely doesn't mean conforming to something that you're not. So much noise has been created by arguing what we are or aren't, who we should or shouldn't be, and what we should or shouldn't do. So. Much. Noise.

But amid it all, we'll find moments of clarity. We'll not waste time arguing. We'll stop distracting ourselves. We'll get in touch with who we are. We'll remember what truly matters. By giving ourselves the time and space, we'll have more of these sacred moments. Eventually, we'll attract more people who help us on the path of being a better person. And then, that one person comes along and helps everything make sense.

More practical tips on communication and how to find your ideal partner are on the way, but with so much division and toxic forms of polarity in our society, everyone needs to know how to work with healthy polarity. There is more news than ever about LGBTQ+ related controversies and it's clearly designed to polarize us and create fights. What comes to mind is a podcast I did with my friend, Kataluna Enriquez, Miss Nevada 2021 and the first trans woman to enter into a Miss USA pageant. What I learned by sitting down with her is that we need to lean into the issues that make us uncomfortable, leaving room for empathy and love. This isn't a fight; it's a chance to get curious.

Ancestral Healing: The Secret to Healthy Romantic Relationships

Polarity is what creates passion. But passion is like fire, so it needs to be balanced with compassion. *Compassion* is the ability to be with someone in their suffering. It's not necessarily doing anything, and definitely not trying to fix each other, but just being fully present. It's beautiful for a masculine man to go fully into his feminine, but he needs to live in his masculine because that's his core essence. As men, we can get in trouble and lose our integrity if we unconsciously live in our feminine, possibly becoming more passive, dependent, and insecure.

At their core, most strong women want to be guided by healthy masculine men. Yet, she only allows it because of the trust that has been built and the safety that's felt. A truly empowered woman doesn't want to be guided by a man who is not embodying a healthy masculine energy because he is not trustworthy, safe, or sturdy. When this dynamic is playing out, a woman will naturally get very frustrated. Anger, frustration, insecurity, and pettiness are not something to use as proof that your partner is miserable to live with—they're signals that something in the foundation of the relationship is unstable and are opportunities for compassion. When one partner starts taking on the masculine (or feminine) roles of the partner, the relationship becomes depolarized. Slowly, or quickly, both parties will become disengaged.

The full power of a woman is to stay in her feminine, but since it's become normalized for men to not take care of their family or abuse the trust placed in them for selfish gain, unfortunately, a lot of women begin living from their masculine.

I get why the "nuclear family" (a family consisting of two parents and their biological children, typically living in one home residence, which is in contrast to a single-parent family or a family with more than two parents) is something many people fear. The previous generations had many toxic, controlling, and abusive marriages, with partners suffering in isolation due to a lack of emotional awareness. Our parents didn't know what we know now. However, with respect and polarity, a traditional family structure is not something to be devalued, dismissed, or degraded.

While I'm personally grateful to have been raised in a nuclear family, I'm even more grateful my mother and father finally separated, due to the hardships and heartbreak they endured in a toxic marriage. Given my father's unfaithfulness and his occasionally harsh behavior toward us, my mom had to put on a masculine shell to protect herself. This robbed my mom of all the things that made her beautiful to me.

I recently sat down with my dad, and we talked for over 8 hours about his childhood and early years of marriage. He gave me the gift of a lifetime to look at his past and understand better why he did the things he did. Being able to reconnect with my dad and understand him better helped me see the blind spots in my own life. This time helped me to love him fully and have empathy where I previously held judgment.

My mom was on the other end of a husband who couldn't hold a safe masculine frame. Because of this, she was unable to provide the nurturing and care that I needed to fully trust the feminine energy in my life. After working through these issues with my own relationship coach, I had a very difficult conversation with my mom. It was important for my own healing to be able to express my truth and talk about what I needed as her son. She is not the villain in the story, she did the best she could. She had no other choice but to put on a masculine shell to protect herself. But the reality remains that this did impact my own relationships with love and connection.

I have a hard time talking about my parents' relationship. Not because of what it was, but because of where they both are now. Together, my parents never had a healthy, polarized relationship, which was common in their generation. Since my dad never made my mom feel safe, she lost the ability to embody feminine love until many years after they divorced. A few years ago, she ended up reuniting with her first love from when she was a teenager—a gentle, beautiful cowboy who is a very healthy, masculine man.

I've been blessed to watch how much softer my mom's gotten in this healthy relationship. The shell she worked for 37 years to build up is finally falling off because she now feels safe. She can stay in her feminine, and it's where she's wanted to be all along. When she told us kids she was going to marry him, it was so beautiful. Crying, she said, "He just makes me feel so special." After years of seeing her hardened, this was one of the most beautiful moments of my life.

This new love in my mom's life allowed us to talk about our relationship with a level of honesty we never could previously. That openness has helped me remove my own insecurities and to begin to trust the love that I receive from women. This is ongoing work, and it's already changed how I show up in dating and trusting women in my life.

We want to believe our parents' love story is more romantic than Jack and Rose on the *Titanic*. They rarely are, and also often end in tragedy. The truth is that my parents probably shouldn't have gotten married. My dad, a lifelong Mormon, felt like he was supposed to, and my mom was a new convert to the church. They weren't crazy in love, nor did they even know if they liked each other. My dad was super pushy, and later, my mom said that she just knew she needed to marry him to have her children.

It didn't take long for them to realize they weren't getting their needs met. Learning about this much later in life, I asked my dad why he stayed in the relationship. For him, it was all about the rules of the church and his beliefs about what was right and wrong. They stayed together for many years, but never shared passionate love.

Learning about their relationship helped me understand more about myself. I did not have parental examples of a healthy masculine or feminine energy. Instead, I had a toxic masculine dad, and most of the time, a mom in self-protection mode who couldn't give the full love she wanted and I needed. The mother of my youth would best be described as "avoidant."

I never saw my parents be affectionate, hold each other, or hold space for each other. But, God bless them, they just didn't have the resources to get it fixed! I don't blame them for anything. I wouldn't change a single thing about who they were because even with all the pain, abuse, lack of freely expressed love, avoidance, and disappointment, I know they did their best with what they had at the time.

When I approached that long conversation with my dad, it wasn't to shame him, blame him, or project my pain onto him— it was just finally time to get clear. As we dug in, I realized there was a lot about him that I'd never heard. His father died when he was 19 years old. Soon after, the family brought another family into their own, causing chaos in their household. Being older than the rest, he was given huge responsibilities, leading him to feel like he let down his siblings. From a young age, he never felt like he was enough.

I asked him when the last time was he shared these hardships with somebody. His response broke my heart, he'd never shared this with anyone. For over 60 years, he never had a place where he could talk about his feelings. No wonder he became toxic! God bless him, how could he be any different without an outlet?

I could have wasted time pointing out all the ways he was hurtful to me, but instead, I went into my feminine polarity and held space for him. The result was deep empathy, compassion, and a newfound sense of respect for the man that helped make me who I am today.

One of the driving reasons why I wanted to write this book and start We Are The They is because this is the book my dad needed. A group like ours would have changed everything for my parents. My dad would have had people to talk to and a place where he was able to express his feelings. He would have been able to move out of a toxic place and find deep satisfaction, connection, and meaning. My mom could have connected with other women, giving her a network of sisters who understood her pain and innate desire to be loved.

The information in this book, and the course that members of We Are The They go through, would have changed everything for them. But they didn't have it, and so unfortunately, they just dealt with things internally. That's why being in a community is so important. My parents had the church, but they couldn't truly be vulnerable there. They had to put on a façade that everything was okay, distorting their authenticity, and ultimately, keeping them out of integrity.

You may not have the opportunity to speak with your parents to find answers. Or maybe you've tried, and it's blown up in your face like it did for me for many years. Whether you actually resolve things with your parents or not, you need a community and oftentimes professional help, to unwind from the pains of the past. If we don't heal from our childhood, our romantic relationships will be reflections of what's not been tended to in our lineage.

If we don't do the work, we'll become the things we hated the most about our own parents. The goal is not to "not be like them" because if we say, feel, or think that, our body just hears "be like them." Instead, it's about finding healthy examples of what we do want to become, examples best found in a loving community. I can promise you this is the perfect preparation you need to attract the partner of your dreams, or if you're in a relationship, exactly what you need to help it thrive.

Be Satisfied

A healthy relationship doesn't only come from what the other person can do for you. Thomas Aquinas said, the highest form of love is to "will the good of the other." Sacrifice is how you know true love is present, but it's not the only ingredient. In romantic relationships, there's a dance between sacrifice and personal sovereignty. You are two individuals, with your own needs, desires, and limits. Yet, the beauty of a relationship is what can be created when you come together.

Focus on the relationship itself and what the interplay between the two of you looks like. Which special characteristics does this relationship have? What brings you and your (ideal) partner together? Close your eyes and imagine how happy you make each other. Envision feeling completely fulfilled and loved by another person. How does that feel? More importantly, why does it feel that way?

Ask yourself what it is that makes this relationship so extraordinary. Can you put it into words? You might not immediately be able to say what makes it feel so special, but it probably has many, if not all, of the characteristics of healthy relationships.

You must hold yourself to high standards if you want a healthy relationship. If your expectations are low and you're not putting in the effort to grow with your partner, the result will be a stale and bad relationship. What is it that you truly want from your relationship? What are the standards you'd hold for yourself and them? What do you expect from your partner, physically and emotionally? These are all things that you need to know for yourself and act on before you can have a healthy relationship.

If you want to maximize the quality of your relationship AND the joy and satisfaction you and your partner have together, then it's time to shift out of a selfish mindset and shift into serving your partner's needs. This starts by being what you want to receive. You have to be loving to get loved. And if you're embodying everything outlined in this book, and they're still criticizing you (or you're criticizing them), then they're likely not the one.

All actions are either two things: giving love or an attempt to be loved. All harm is caused when seeking to be loved, and all healing happens in a state of giving love. Only in a state of empathy, compassion, and openness can someone truly receive love.

There is nothing more intimate, nor any situation that brings out more of our fears or insecurities, than a romantic relationship. When you demonstrate how to be a better partner by practicing empathy rather than heightening your partner's angst, you step up and embrace the opportunity for connection.

Conflict Resolution Practice

To close this chapter, consider this practice that reestablishes polarity, trust, and passion in a relationship. This practice has two roles: The Speaking Partner (the one who feels triggered), who follows the five steps, and the Listening Partner (the one holding space). It's ideal to allow time between switching roles if both partners have triggers they want to address.

To have an extraordinary romantic relationship, follow these five steps:

1. **Express Your Feeling:** This is about sharing how you feel as concisely as possible. For example, "I feel disrespected right now." Please note that it's never framed as, "I feel that you did XYZ."
2. **Express Your Desire:** Share what you want or need in the relationship. For example, "I desire to feel connected and loved."
3. **State or Clarify Boundaries:** Make it clear what you will not tolerate, such as, "I will not accept being spoken to in that tone."
4. **Sacred Ask:** The Speaking Partner makes one specific request that the Listening Partner must do their best to agree to. This could be a behavioral agreement like "no yelling when fighting"

or a request for better communication about daily or weekly schedules.

5. **Physically Connect:** As soon as both parties feel safe and in integrity, they should try to connect physically. This re-establishes physical intimacy and reinforces the connection between partners. I promise, this is one of the best times to have sex because when you make up in complete integrity with each other, there's no weird lingering energy, and you both will be as polarized as possible.

By following this process, it creates a space where you can express emotions, set boundaries, and make requests in a respectful and caring way. Remember, it might be helpful to allow time for both partners to switch roles and work through their triggers, practicing patience and empathy throughout the process. Or, if needed, a third party or relationship counseling professional can mediate the Conflict Resolution Practice.

Bonus Chapter

1

Find One

From SKEPTICAL to TRUSTING

"The flower doesn't dream of the bee. It blossoms and the bee comes."
—Mark Nepo

MAYBE IT IS true that men are from Mars and women are from Venus. We're so different, right? No, not really. We all come from the same place—the womb of our mothers—and we're all stewards of the Earth. Together, we truly are all one. But thank God for variety. What a hellish world it would be if everyone looked, spoke, thought, and acted exactly like we do.

Many of us are destined to look for *the* one—the person that's uniquely different from us, yet similar enough to be compatible. Finding *the* one can take years, filled with heartbreak and sadness, and occasional moments of semi-satisfaction. Many a John just settle with a Jane because it's easier than the search. Marriage becomes a contractual obligation, a duty to fulfill, and a task to accomplish. Like my parents and millions of others, good things can still come from this kind of relationship.

But that's not soul-satisfying love. That light-your-world-on-fire, drop-everything-to-see-them, pure-joy-every-time-they-walk-through-the-door, and everything-up-until-you-met-them-just-makes-perfect-sense kind of love. If you're like me and have had your heart broken, multiple times, it's easy to be skeptical that this kind of love is real and can be sustained. When you see it, you think to yourself, "No, they're just faking it because they're out in public." "Will I ever find my soulmate? Oh, what the hell am I even talking about? Soulmates aren't real."

A lot of us are born into families and into a society where it disconnects us from receiving love or being free to give love. But as we age and mature, we can stay disconnected, causing us to seek out and get into unfulfilling relationships. When a woman is not free to express the depth of her love or a man has been shamed for being vulnerable, it's easy to stay in a shallow place.

If you're not looking to find the one or make your current relationship 10 times better, this isn't the book for you. But I think you are. In that case, you have to embody a frequency that will attract the right people into your life. If you're unclear with what you want, you'll meet a thousand different revolving door options that aren't the right fit. You end up finding all the other people who are exactly where you are, causing you to miss out on quality and depth. There's a better way.

What Every Woman Wants

Women and men need to be free to cry, express their pain, and make a mess. When a woman cries, it lowers the testosterone levels of her male partner so he's able to soften and hold space. A healthy, strong woman has nothing to fear when her male partner feels safe enough to open his heart and let the tears roll. The beauty of crying is that you can fully go into it knowing it's not going to last forever. But if you hold on to tears, it keeps toxic stress hormones repressed in your body. It's said that saltwater heals, whether it's swimming in the ocean, salinated water for maximum hydration, or shedding tears. I know it would be a less toxic world if everyone felt safe and free to simply be.

Whether you're a man or a woman, the freedom to just be yourself is how you know you're in the presence of people who love you. However, for thousands of years, women have been told how to dress, when to speak, what to look like, and even more destructive, that just being themselves was not okay.

The fundamental wound for most men is the feeling like we'll never be enough. For most women, it's the fear that they're too much. Too loud, too intense, too expressive—that fundamentally, their existence is wrong, and they need to fix it.

What nearly every woman wants is the freedom to just be. Some days she may be flowing like a river, trickling like a creek, or crushing like a tidal wave. What she wants is the freedom to flow, and when she does become more intense, her partner holds their strong boundaries, not shaming her or trying to change her, but allowing her to be seen, felt, and protected amid it all.

For many men, our impulse is to fix or figure out, and I can tell you from learning the hard way, this is not what most women want. Well, after the tidal wave subsides, she asks for perspective, that's the only time it will be fully received. The truth is that it's the most masculine thing possible to not "fix" the situation or try to control her. Weak men will read this and think it's beta behavior to do what I'm recommending. Women don't care what weak men think, they just want unconditional love from a strong man.

For a woman to fully be in her feminine, it requires confidence to do so. In a way, this means she has to be confident in her own masculine energy to know that she's going to be okay, regardless of how a man responds. This allows her to be free of depending on a man's masculine energy to feel safe in the world. But, once she finds a man who can meet her with his own healthy masculine energy, she can fully relax into and trust her feminine polarity. However, if a man keeps responding badly, she has no obligation to stick around to be used or abused.

That's not to say people are disposable and that you should bounce the moment things get hard. Conflict is a great opportunity for growth. But if a man exhibits toxic masculine behaviors, like trying to fix, change, shame, or dismiss, then that queen is keeping the door closed for her true king to join her.

Where to Find One

If you want to find a good guy, you have to go to places where the motivated guys are. Go to self-development events, the gym early in the morning, church, community outreach events, or business seminars. I'm sure there are a million love stories of meeting someone in a bar, at a concert, or on a bachelor(ette) trip, but I recommend keeping your expectations low if looking for *the* one at those kinds of places. The pitfall of going to parties to find your person is that the people who are attracted there are immersed in a world of stimulus and excitement. Also, if you're even there, it's likely a sign you're not really ready for what you think you want.

I know what it's like to be in the party scene because for years I was running them. I was known across the entire state of Utah for throwing the biggest parties with the most beautiful people. With NBA All-Stars on speed dial and the sway to throw parties with epic girl-to-guy ratios, I could definitely draw interest. It wasn't unusual for someone to brag about a party they had been to, not even knowing I was the one who hosted it. While fun and full of epic stories, I wasn't ever going to get serious with anyone while living that lifestyle. I felt so uncomfortable in my body when I tried to genuinely connect because I was used to the stimulus of having so many people around. Clearly, this kind of environment is not conducive to somebody who's wanting to root down and grow deeply with one person.

After a while, the party lifestyle left me feeling empty and longing for depth. I had a broad reach, but what I really wanted was somebody close who truly knew my soul. You're not going to get that closeness, or even feel comfortable in your own skin, until you do the work to overcome that dependence. Some couples that met at parties continue that lifestyle because it's all that they know. They usually end up in trouble because they're not accessing true depth with one another.

Dating apps are another area full of landmines. From a guy's standpoint, it often feels as though the system is stacked against us. This can seriously damage our confidence, leading to a feeling of continual rejection. In reality, many women aren't even seeing your profile, and the statistics reveal a significant disparity in the number of women who swipe right compared to men.

For women, dating apps can create a distorted sense of self-worth. With countless men showing interest, it might seem flattering at first. But most women desire to be appreciated for more than just their appearance, and these platforms are predicated on looks. As a result, you may attract the very type of individuals you wish to avoid—those who only value physical appearances. When looks are the initial draw, it's easy to end up connecting with shallow individuals or those whose priorities are misaligned with your own.

Since these apps prioritize convenience, they attract those who are likely to put in minimal effort. Those who rely solely on apps are less willing to approach someone in person, fight for a relationship, or work hard to maintain it. To them, options are plentiful, and people become expendable. These dynamics make the dating app experience a net loss for everyone involved—except for the tech company, of course.

The notion that people are expendable is a huge source of toxicity in our culture. Every extraordinary relationship has intention behind it. Personally, when I was using dating apps, or over-using social media, it wasn't based on intention. It was all about *attention*. I was caught up in the game, concerned with who was available right now, rather than who might be the right person for me.

During a digital detox, I realized that most of my behavior was driven by the desire for a dopamine hit. That's what these apps are fundamentally about. By keeping the attention of multiple women at once, the underlying motivation was the thrill of validation, not genuine interest. I was merely seeking to be affirmed, not truly engaging with them, and that's what these platforms encourage. It's a cycle that depolarizes your energy and blocks you from forming meaningful connections.

We use things and others for our own selfish, short-term benefits rather than to do the work to cultivate a deep soul satisfaction. We do this because the more someone really sees you, the more of a chance they have to break your heart. It's the most courageous thing in the world to open your heart, your life, your mind, your body, and desires to someone. No wonder why so many people stay numb, overstimulated, guarded, and skeptical. But all it takes is the choice to do the work needed to start making better decisions, surrounding yourself with great people, and you'll attract exactly who's meant for you.

We're now officially in the era where most Americans meet their spouse online. However, over 30% of people still find their spouse through a mutual friend or family member, and those who do are the least likely to get divorced within 10 years. This speaks to the power of communities and the importance of surrounding yourself with the right people. By connecting with those who share your values, both male and female, you expand your world, attracting others who can help you find *the* one. Being a part of a community like *We Are The They* is what gives you opportunities that can make your dreams come true.

What to Look for in a Guy

If you want to be in a relationship, you need to find someone that's ready to be in a relationship. Seems self-evident, but we all know what it's like to be played by someone who's "hard to get." You need to know if they have space in their life for the kind of relationship you want. Are they making the choices of someone who's ready to be in a serious relationship?

Before offering traits of good guys, it's worth noting that most men are afraid to be vulnerable. However, creating and inviting a man into a safe space where he can truly open up is how you'll win over his heart. Many women find it challenging to be vulnerable themselves, but they naturally hold space well. However, the downside of this inclination is pleasing and appeasing a man by holding space for immature behaviors. That's unhealthy. Just because a woman is capable of holding space doesn't mean she needs to be a man's only place of refuge. If a woman is vulnerable and a man takes advantage of that, he has some serious work to do. Sometimes all it takes is a clear request from a strong woman and a good man will hear her and trust going through the process of opening up.

Here's what to look for in a guy. A man of integrity will be upfront, honest, and consistent. He's going to do what he says he's going to do. He's confident in his own decision-making, so he's not easily persuaded. He knows what he wants and works for it. He will be clear about the people he wants in his life, and he'll have high-quality friendships with men and unsuspicious friendships with women. He may not have perfect relationships with his parents, but it will be clear he doesn't harbor resentment or blame them for anything.

A good man is nonjudgmental, but he has good judgment. He doesn't willingly put himself in danger, yet he's not afraid to do difficult things. A man of integrity knows that service is his greatest calling, but he doesn't diminish or lose himself in the process. To find a great man with a good heart, look for one who doesn't attempt to kill off his ego, isn't afraid to explore the shadows, but unquestionably lives in the light of humility, grace, kindness, gentleness, and self-control.

If a man is in integrity, he'll embody the 5 Pillars of Success. This means he'll make good decisions and take strong moral stands. He'll have behaviors that show his true, loving, playful, and confident sense of self. He'll have great friends and be a great friend. He'll be consistent and accountable, and he'll also have mentors who support and guide him deeper into integrity. If you're getting to know a man, observe who he looks up to. Who are they following? Are the people they attract the kind of people you want in your world?

Another green flag is a man who's able to hold space and be in his feminine receptivity, and has the strength that it takes to be soft. A big red flag is a guy who is secretive, not willing to change, or is sneaky with his phone or social media. Is he in the moment or is his attention always somewhere else? Are you the light of his life, or just another trophy for the mantle? Does he revere you as the goddess you are, or does his wandering eyes erode the foundation of what could be a healthy relationship? You know you have a keeper if he can be fully present with you.

Be Trusting

Men are mysterious. We like to play hard, but we also know to pray harder. We make mistakes, but we know how to build on them, making something majestic out of the most mundane. We have a fire inside us that fuels us to work hard, lead others, and be a way-maker in tough times. We can be intense, but what we really want is to have loved ones and a valuable life that's worth fighting for and protecting. We can joke that we come from Mars, but our deepest strength and resilience stems from a universal force: God-given strength, wisdom, and a heart for service.

What are the unspoken things that are really going on in a man's heart? We want to be respected, cherished, and we need to know that we matter. A man wants to know that he's needed in your life and that you see something special in him. He wants to feel like he has a purpose and that he truly matters to others, and especially to you. He wants to know that you have his back, no matter what, literally through thick or thin. It's a nonnegotiable for him to know he can be real with you without having to pretend that he's always at his best.

When a woman gives a man a safe space, he will show up for her in every way, shape, and form. A woman embodying unconditional love and a man being entirely present will both know they're treasured. That's a relationship for the ages.

Bonus Chapter

2

Raise One

From SELF-CONSCIOUS to SELF-AWARE

"He didn't tell me how to live. He lived and let me watch him do it."
                                                              —Mel Abraham

ON ONE OF my many houseboat trips to Lake Powell, I happened to
see my three scout leaders from when I was a kid. All these years,
they stayed friends. I approached and unexpectedly got emotional,
telling them how grateful I was for the time and effort they poured
into me. Now that I'm over 40 years old, I can appreciate how these
men had families and worries of their own. As a kid, I took them for
granted, not realizing the sacrifice it took to take us camping and
spend entire weeks with us during the summer. I didn't always make
it easy for them, yet they were so patient and kind, helping shape
me into the person I am today.

When we're kids, we don't realize our elders have their own
concerns. Some of my scout leaders were probably fighting with
their wives, dealing with health issues or tragedies, and the same
things I've gone through. Nevertheless, they showed up and gave us
kids their love, attention, and intention. They didn't have to, but
they did. With the Next Gen group of We Are The They, a program
that has a lot of the same elements as my main program only
designed for teens, I'm able to give back in similar ways. Giving
teens and parents the tools they need to build confidence in their
children, and in their own parenting.

Raising a person of integrity is what's needed to grow deep roots
and withstand the toxicity that pervades our world. Teens live in a
climate like we've never known. In some ways, they're more self-
aware than we were at their age, but they're also more self-conscious
due to harmful impacts of social media and entertainment. It's our
sacred responsibility to uphold standards of virtue and goodness
while also respecting their individuality. The most important thing
every teen needs is community. Hyper-individualism is a byproduct

of American society, but it leaves us lost, alone, and disconnected. The right kind of community will be a lifesaver for them and for you.

What Every Kid Wants

A few hours into the first day of the Next Gen program, I say, "Raise your hand if you wish you were closer to your mom and dad." Usually, all but one or two raise their hand. Keep in mind, almost all of the parents of these kids are active in We Are The They, meaning they've been truly working on themselves. Still, their kids want a closer relationship. While I trust wholeheartedly that you're applying what's been offered in this book, there's a 90% chance that your child wants to feel more connected to you.

Most parents and teens aren't having essential one-on-one talks or the occasional tough conversation, leading to a lack of deep connection. During a recent conversation with my dad, I realized it wasn't a lack of desire to connect vulnerably that kept us apart but rather a lack of skills. Unfortunately, many parents don't possess the skills needed to have these vital conversations with their kids. Many parents are afraid to talk to their children, not because they fear the answers, but simply because they don't know how. They remain on the surface since they don't know how to hold space or ask deeper questions.

What parents really need, and what their children desire, is a deeper understanding of each other. It's similar to relationships with women, where communication might not be direct, but it's essential to learn and comprehend their nonverbal and subtle language. Otherwise, the connection might always be lacking. Children have their own unique way of communicating, and parents must be willing to tap into their language to truly connect. For kids in the Next Gen program, I engage in side conversations to help crack them open by asking deeper questions and encouraging them to express their emotions. By asking them how certain experiences made them feel and talking about things that were relevant to them, they knew I understood them on a more genuine level.

A buddy told me that he and his 14-year-old daughter were clashing nonstop. She was always on TikTok, and he said their relationship was the worst it had ever been. So, I asked him, "Have you ever sat down next to her and asked why she loves TikTok?" He quickly let me know how much he hated it and how bad it is for her, so no, he'd never used it as a point of connection.

Picture being her or someone her age. Everyone at school uses it, it's entertaining, and by the way, TikTok is hilarious. It knows exactly what you think is funny, and they'll show it to you all day. His daughter, and millions of children, are dealing with something that we never had to—the most addictive attention grabber that's ever hit the market.

I advised my buddy to see it from her perspective. Every time he walked in the room, what would happen? She would get a sick feeling in her gut since she knew he disapproved of what she's doing. She'd feel guilty and ashamed, which would naturally just drive her further away and make her inclined to use the app, something that seemed to make her feel good. I told my friend, "Next time she's on her phone, sit down and say: Alright, I need to see what's so cool about TikTok. Show me your favorite ones."

He took my advice, and it changed everything. Instead of hiding or pulling away from him, what used to drive them apart became a point of connection. Now that he's regained trust, he can guide and teach his daughter lessons because she knows her dad understands. Since he couldn't grasp the basics, like why his child enjoyed TikTok, they were missing out on the deeper things going on in their life.

A concerned mother once told me her athletic son, who had a great life, recently became very depressed. I immediately suspected it was about a girl, and I was right. She was shocked that I knew, but I reminded her I had been a teenager once. She didn't know how to approach the subject with her son. I explained to her that people, especially kids, will open up when they feel understood without judgment. I recommended for her to say something like, "Hey, I don't know exactly what's going on in your world, but when I was 14, something similar happened to me, and it really sucked." By leading with vulnerability instead of trying to parent them or change their behavior, it shows understanding and helps them feel more at ease. It's about making them feel that they're not alone and knowing that someone truly comprehends what they're going through.

Another friend was concerned about his 15-year-old son who had started sneaking around, smoking weed, and getting into trouble. Devastated by his son's action, he knew he'd never get into Harvard by being on this path. Confused, I asked him if that's what his son wanted, only to find out that my friend hadn't asked. My friend, who respects my opinion, seemed to need a reminder of my own path, which included mistakes in my teens and twenties, but ultimately allowed me to find my voice. I explained that I'd gone to junior college, not Harvard, and that my dad had given me the freedom to figure things out on my own. I asked him to consider, "What if my dad had needed me to go to an Ivy League school and I never got to just become me?" He was taken aback by this perspective.

It's essential to not impose our own egos on our children's futures. Instead of needing them to satisfy our own desires, provide them with tools to grow their integrity, while giving them the freedom to choose what they want in life. This doesn't mean allowing them to eat candy and play video games all day. But pain in life comes from unmet expectations, so it's essential to find out what they want and support them with healthy ambitions instead of ego-based expectations. My friend, taking this advice to heart, discovered his son's interest in sports and other activities. By leaning into those interests and offering support and love regardless of "failure," they were able to rebuild a strong relationship.

What every child wants isn't that different from what we want. Every person, especially someone who's still growing and forming their sense of self (you included), wants these four things:

- To be heard.
- To be seen.
- To be valued.
- To be loved.

As a parent, it's your responsibility to create the conditions for these four things for yourself and your kids. Healthy friendships and relationships make these four possible. And when you feel heard, seen, valued, and loved, you can pour those things into others.

How You Treat Your Inner Child Is How You'll Treat Your Children

If you have a child or wish you could go back to when you were 14 years old, this is the most important thing to remember: you can be the person that your younger self needed and wanted. We all remember what it was like to be a kid. In those moments when we fell down and were crying, when we were getting into trouble, weren't making good decisions, or when we wanted to be heard, what did we need? To have a resilient parent, role model, or elder remind us that we were safe, loved, and capable.

To raise healthy, resilient children, all you have to do is tap into the thought, "What would I have wanted as a young person, and what can I offer now as an adult?" Giving your child, or your own inner child, this care and attention breaks the cycle of negative behavior. It shifts you out of reactivity and into receptivity. Anyone can perpetuate a cycle, but it only takes one to break it.

Our children are reflections of the things that we haven't healed, and they trigger us perfectly. Anything that hasn't been tended to within a relationship will manifest in the children they have together. If a kid is struggling with something, that means that the parents are struggling with it too. Parents can rise to the challenge, heal themselves, and hold themselves to the same high standard they expect of their kids. This is such a sneaky thing because someone can say, "I want my kid to do better than me." It sounds virtuous, but often, it's about the parents' ego. Sneaky pride and an untended inner child are what perpetuates unhealthy generational patterns.

Parents should shift their focus from pinpointing what their children are doing wrong to recognizing and praising what they're doing right. When you acknowledge a positive behavior, it encourages them to do more of it, and this in turn builds their confidence.

True parental confidence means allowing children to become who they are meant to be, rather than shaping them to fulfill the parent's desires or sense of achievement. Unfortunately, some parents may project their own lack of confidence onto their children. But this is about the parent, not the child. When you guide children with integrity and confidence, you don't impose your own needs on them. As the wise Solomon said, "Train a child in the way that he should go, and when he is older, he will not turn from it."

Be Self-Aware

When communicating and teaching our children, we must show them that we are competent adults whom they can trust. The key here is for the child to see their parents living a passionate and fulfilling life. If they witness that, they'll want to model their life after their parents. They'll think, "My dad has a fantastic life. I want to be like him. I'll listen to what he says." But if the father appears miserable and constantly fights with his wife, complains about finances, or talks badly about his own friends, any sane child will think, "Why should I listen to my dad? His life is a mess."

Create a life that your children admire. When they see you excited about your life, they will want to emulate it, and they'll be receptive to your guidance and the deep conversations that build connection, love, and closeness.

9

Be the King

From IRRELEVANT to APPRECIATED

"I am indeed a king because I know how to rule myself."

—Pietro Arentino

GOOD MEN NEED to know how to lead and build things of value that are aligned with positive visions. If they do not, evil men will fill in that void. Part of your responsibility is to help inspire, lead, and guide others so that you can make our world a better place for everyone. For you to be able to lead and have genuine impact, you need to know how to show up properly as a respected man.

In this chapter, you'll learn how to truly appreciate yourself and gain the respect of those around you. It starts by embodying the insights of the previous chapters, yet you must also understand the social dynamics that happen in daily interactions. By fully knowing your natural behaviors, strengths, and weaknesses, you'll be able to show up in big ways and be attuned to the subtleties that most people miss. Do you know how to treat others the way they want to be treated? Do you know how to speak so that people listen? Do people jump at the opportunity to help you when you need something to get done? You will and they will.

For the past 20 years, I've been in rooms with some of the most influential humans on the planet. I did so methodically and with intention. I knew how to genuinely connect, create value, and win them over. I wasn't just getting invited to the table, I was consistently the guy they wanted to get to know. Leadership, appreciation, and value creation can all be taught and learned, but it's up to you to apply it. Ever feel like if you walked into a room or out of it nobody would care? I'll teach you every insight and social cue I know so feeling irrelevant will be a thing of the past. You'll step into your future feeling appreciated from within, and then by everyone around you.

Every day you sell your family, friends, or colleagues on what you want them to do for you or with you. To be in healthy agreements

173

with everyone around you, it's important to have skill sets to lead with confidence, conviction, and compassion. By learning how to show up correctly—how to be the king of your own life—you can influence everyone you come into contact with for the benefit of all.

Lean into Your Leadership—The World Needs It

What leadership truly entails is only learned through experience. It's not about motivation or creating ideals that you convince people to attain. It's understanding human behavior, and the irrefutable fact that you can't change anybody. All you can do is create the space and opportunity for changes to take place, and then inspire them to change themselves. My entire coaching program is predicated on members knowing what they need to do. If they know what they need to do, but keep repeating ineffective, negative, or toxic behaviors, there's no formula, tool, or technique that will "fix" them. I've had people very close to me for decades, and no matter what I say or do, they simply will not change. But in our program, men, their wives, and teens are supported on every level so that changing becomes inevitable.

Few people know what the key to behavioral change really is. If you want to change your behaviors and create new, healthy habits, what's the key? Repetition? Consistency? Yes, but there's something that has to happen first. If you want your new positive behaviors to last, you must have an identity change. An identity change simply means seeing yourself embodying who you want to become, and then aligning your behaviors and lifestyle as an emanation of your new identity.

Trying to force change on someone, or shaming them into change, is a frustrating and fruitless experience. All you can do is show them another way and support them in having an identity change to become a more authentic version of themself.

Your job as a parent, boss, or a leader of any kind is to inspire others and show them that they can have something different with their life. Along with offering insights and new ways of thinking, being a leader includes teaching the skills mentees need to utilize. And the best way to teach? To be. Leaders teach by being the example of what's possible. The way to lose all credibility as a leader is the philosophy of, "Do as I say but not as I do." Sadly, many people operate this way and achieve some semblance of success. But if a leader is telling people to do something, but they're not doing it, they're playing a very finite game. Once the truth is revealed, their leadership becomes irrelevant.

Look at the toxic state of leadership in our country. We have extreme problems because so few people of integrity aspire to be politicians. Collectively, we don't trust them anymore because they say one thing and then do another. When COVID lockdowns were at their peak in California, the governor, medical lobbyists, and other politicians were caught in an enclosed space with no social distancing or masks being worn all while enforcing statewide mandates for the public. That's the opposite of a true leader. Or, at the peak of some of the worst storms in Texas, leading to millions being without power and in freezing cold homes, their longtime senator jetted off to Cancun. A leader shows up, alongside you, and doesn't leave until the job is done. It's leading from the front when the easiest option is to run away.

I have a tattoo of a Spartacus sword on my finger because that's my alter ego. I love Spartacus because he was the first one to run into the fight—he was leading from the front. You can only lead people to do the work as much as you've done it for yourself. The second you start talking about what you're going to do, you have no credibility to lead other people. A true leader says, "I know where you're at, and I know where you're trying to go. I've been there. So, watch this, get on my back, and I'm going to teach you how to do it." They love you and they inspire you to want to do it. Think of the lead characters in inspiring movies like *Shawshank Redemption*, *Gladiator*, or *Braveheart*. It's not just what they said, it's who those leaders were.

True leaders are doing the work themselves, so they must have the freedom to be wrong. One of the biggest mistakes a leader can make is acting like they doesn't make any. I definitely don't act like I'm infallible. When I lead, sometimes I fall. For example, I make everyone in our coaching program agree to never make one of the other men look bad. Unfortunately, on one of our trips to Hawaii, I made a joke about one of the guys who was out surfing in front of his wife and some other guys. I instantly realized that what I said could make him look bad.

I pulled him and his wife aside about 30 minutes later and told him what I'd done, and apologized. I was devastated, and even started to get emotional. I had made one of my brothers look small, something I absolutely shouldn't have done. There were no excuses made; I was completely wrong. It was a reflection of my own insecurities and bad habits from the past. He offered me a hug, turning what felt like a negative situation into a moment of understanding. He showed me that leadership isn't about never making mistakes, but owning them when they occur. In that moment, he knew he could trust me because even if I made a mistake, he knew I would own it.

Leaders often make the mistake of trying never to show vulnerability, refusing to let others see that they are human. But being relatable is vital. If you watch the documentary *Mitt* on Netflix, you'll find Mitt Romney very likable and relatable. But that wasn't the impression he gave when running for president nor when I had him on my podcast. During his campaign, he came off as an elitist, making comments about how people who were dependent on the government would never vote for someone like him.

Humans are generally forgiving, allowing space for mistakes. That's why some political figures have had so much success; people are okay with mistakes as long as you are willing to own them and apologize. However, those who don't take responsibility don't find forgiveness. When Lance Armstrong was caught doping, he attacked his teammates and only came clean when he had no other options. To this day, he has not gotten back into the sporting world's good graces.

On the other hand, we admire figures like Tiger Woods, who made major mistakes but owned them. When he won the Masters in 2019, it was hailed as one of the greatest moments in sports history. We love a good redemption story, and we love a comeback. Good-natured people are quick to forgive if you own your mistakes and move on. That's what a leader does; they own their actions, learn from them, and become symbols of resilience and authenticity.

Everyone Deserves to Be Heard

A great example of different styles of leadership happened just last summer, in August 2023 when I took over 50 guys in WATT to Lake Powell. As you may have noticed reading this far into the book, boathouse trips to the lake have been the most consistent excursion I've done throughout my life. While I am no boating master, I have a considerable amount of experience, as did many of the other guys (which is an important detail for this story).

We anchored at a beach that had a lot of other houseboats along the shore, but within a few hours, a huge storm kicked in around 6:00 at night. All of our anchors were coming out of our houseboat, and it was an all-hands-on-deck situation. Our boat started heading straight to this giant yacht of a houseboat, one of the nicest boats you can get on the lake. We had over 40 guys on the ropes, I was on the engine, and the people from the other boat, that we were on a crash-course toward, jumped out and started helping us.

One guy, in particular, who had the body of a gladiator and was jacked out of his mind, ran over and was screaming at everyone. He was helping like none other to dig new anchor holes, but he was also name-calling, belittling everyone, and leading with a certain kind of energy I've experienced many times throughout my life. The high winds and the torrential storm made for an intense situation, but his attitude made it even more tense.

Eventually, once we got our boat tied down, he came up to me and asked who was the leader of this huge group of "inept, unmanly men." He was poised to fight me, and any other time in my life, this guy would have completely triggered me. I would have gone after him, but my blood pressure didn't raise a single percent. Calmly, I thanked him for how essential it was that he dug those holes, pointing out it was not lost on me how hard he worked to help us out. I pointed out that he probably saved us, and without his actions, we'd be in an even more inconvenient situation.

And then, doing my best to show a different kind of leadership, I said, "I have 40 guys out here. They're not all boat guys, but at the end of the day, we were all on the ropes. I don't think it's a masculinity problem that we couldn't dig the anchors, but we made sure the houseboat didn't get swept away. Plus, I've been on this beach with some of the most masculine men alive and watched their houseboats flip on their side. Sometimes a storm like this just blows in." He wasn't having any logical or kind thing I had to say, so he continued to berate me saying we shouldn't have parked so close and continuing to make it clear he didn't respect us.

I let him know that we were going to do a big breathwork session the next day, so we needed the beach, and I also pointed out that all the other houseboats were much closer than ours were. He stormed off mid-conversation, but an hour later, he came back over. Visibly upset with himself, he started apologizing. He told me that for the last few years, he'd been working hard on bettering himself, but seeing us guys all together triggered him. While I appreciated his apology, he was still too caught up in his shame to really be open for resolution, within himself and with us.

The next morning, he came back over and told me how he didn't sleep all night. He said, "I received so many lessons from yesterday, but it's been a long road for me to get here. I used to be 250 pounds, was an alcoholic, and was suicidal." He started crying, telling me how he discovered a book that changed his life. It was about how to be a better man and what healthy masculinity looks like. He continued on, saying, "I looked up your guys' website, and you all are doing the exact things that I did to turn my life around. I should be teaching others like you, but instead, I'm over here calling you guys names and being a complete jerk."

His vulnerability and authentic apology moved me, and after hearing his story and clearing the air, he went back to his boat. About 30 minutes later, a few of my guys and I had an idea to invite him to come speak to our group. We had a couple other speakers lined up already, but I wanted all of the guys to hear his story. He agreed and told us all about his transformation, highlighting how yoga and eating healthy completely changed his life. The most beautiful part was that he brought his 14-year-old daughter so she could witness him get teary eyed and emotional and talking about his transformation.

Afterward, I gave him a big hug and asked for him to lead us in a yoga session the next morning. Needless to say, we've become really good friends, and he loves everything about WATT and what we're doing. Any other time in my life, I probably would have called that guy an asshole, yelled at him, and we would have had this weird energy on the beach. We would not have been able to have a comfortable breathwork session because we would have been worried about the music pissing him off. Instead, we had a beautiful experience where everyone got to see the contrast of toxic versus healthy masculinity.

He would have triggered me with everything he was doing if I hadn't done the work. Instead, I got to see him as the man, beyond his actions. Like Brené Brown talks about, anytime you really lean into somebody, it's hard not to love them. Once I heard his story, I saw he was just having a bad moment instead of assuming he was a miserable human. By allowing him to have his moment, in the long term, we all got to have a beautiful experience, which ended up being my favorite part of the entire weekend.

The 4 Behavioral Styles

An effective leader understands and effectively utilizes behaviors to their advantage. ***However, we cannot lead others until we lead ourselves***. The 4 Behavioral Styles is a behavioral assessment tool that categorizes individuals into one of four different behavioral styles: Dominance (D), Influence (I), Steadiness (S), and Conscientiousness (C). Understanding these styles cannot only help us know HOW we do something, but also WHY we do things. By identifying strengths, weaknesses, motivations, and communication styles, we can lead ourselves and others with confidence. When we understand ourselves, we can communicate more effectively with our spouse, children, employees, and clients.

The 4 Behavioral Styles and their associated characteristics are:

1. **Dominance (D):**
   - How They Do Things: Driven, assertive, and goal oriented.
   - Why They Do Things: To achieve results and overcome challenges.
   - Example: A leader with a strong D style pushes their team to meet tight deadlines.
   - How to Lean into This Style: Focus on results, set clear goals, and challenge yourself and others to meet them. When a situation requires strong decision-making and swift actions, this is when to harness this behavior.

2. **Influence (I):**
   - How They Do Things: Enthusiastic, optimistic, and lively.
   - Why They Do Things: To collaborate with others and create an enjoyable environment.
   - Example: An individual with an I style thrives in team collaboration and networking events.
   - How to Lean into This Style: Emphasize relationships, foster a positive environment, and use your influence to motivate others. This is particularly effective in team-building and negotiation scenarios.

3. **Steadiness (S):**
   - How They Do Things: Calm, patient, and consistent.
   - Why They Do Things: To provide support, maintain stability, and create harmony.
   - Example: A manager with an S style is a go-to person for support and guidance within a team.
   - How to Lean into This Style: Cultivate patience, show empathy, and foster a cooperative environment. This behavior style is beneficial when nurturing long-term relationships, and maintaining a balanced and stable work environment.

4. **Conscientiousness (C):**
   - How They Do Things: Precise, analytical, and detail-oriented.
   - Why They Do Things: To ensure accuracy, quality, and adherence to standards.
   - Example: A C-style individual excels in quality control, long-term projects, and research positions.
   - How to Lean into This Style: Focus on facts, adhere to standards, and carefully analyze decisions. This is valuable in scenarios requiring critical analysis, problem-solving, and adherence to high standards.

Understanding these behavioral styles and their interplay gives you an effective blueprint to motivate, guide, and collaborate with others. By harnessing your own behavioral style and understanding the styles of those around you, you'll lead with greater confidence and insight, creating harmony within any environment.

Be the Observed, Not the Observer

A decade ago, I ended an engagement and re-entered the singles scene in my local town. I didn't know anyone but wanted to quickly get plugged back in. I decided to join a group of 200 singles doing a three-day houseboat trip to Lake Powell. I knew I would get lost in the crowd and not make many new friends if I didn't plan accordingly.

I used a principle a mentor had taught me, "Be the observed, not the observer." With that in mind, I decided to drive out of my way to buy a bunch of Roman candles (fireworks that shoot out like small cannons). I was going to get guys to have a Roman candle war. I had experimented with this before, and it was always such a hit.

On the last night, I announced this to all the guys and challenged them to war. I gave 20 different men two Roman candles each. I also only had two Roman candles, but I knew something they didn't. Each of theirs shot 10 flaming balls, one at a time. The two I had shot over 200, rapid fire like a machine gun!

I got hit once or twice, but I absolutely unloaded on these guys, and they were all hit at least five times. It was just as epic as I had hoped. Everyone laughed until we cried, with burn marks for days and a story for a lifetime. After that experience, everyone wanted to know me, talk to me, and see what I was about. I had been borderline invisible for two days, yet after that night, I had dozens of new connections who all had a good reason to come up and talk to me.

One of the worst parts of the internet and social media is how many people waste their lives watching other people live theirs. Being a watcher is being on the outside. It's window shopping instead of buying, valuing, and having the damn thing. It's watching porn alone in a cold, dark room instead of experiencing reality. Watchers are close enough to know what's happening, but not on the inside really experiencing the fullness of life.

Be someone who is willing to put yourself out there. "You miss 100% of the shots you don't take" isn't just word salad. Be an active participant in everything you do. You may learn something by observing, but you develop skills, gain experience, and garner respect by being the observed.

Choose Your Battles Wisely, King

For this next story, I want you to be on the lookout for two different things: 1) the power of making intelligent decisions with no emotion, and 2) what a true leader does when faced with a common problem.

Last year, in my area of town, a tragic road rage incident resulted in the death of a father of three children, who, by all accounts, seemed to be a decent man. The incident began when another driver cut him off multiple times on the freeway. In a moment of poor judgment that anyone might have succumbed to, the two drivers signaled to each other to pull off the road and confronted each other. Once they parked, the situation quickly escalated. The father approached the other vehicle and slammed the driver's windshield in anger. In response, the other driver pulled out a gun. As the father tried to wrestle the gun away, the driver shot him in the chest, killing him instantly. This story is more than a cautionary tale; it's a profound tragedy. Not only were two lives ruined in that brief moment of rage, but hundreds of other lives were permanently affected by the loss.

Several years ago, I began training to go undercover with Operation Underground Railroad, the organization behind the popular movie *The Sound of Freedom*. We took extensive Krav Maga training multiple times per week. This form of fighting is different from martial arts because it's basically doing whatever you can to end the fight and go home to your family. The first rule they ever taught us was if there is any way possible to avoid the fight, then do so. The only reason to learn how to fight in the first place is so, hopefully, you never have to.

Around this time, I saw a video by a friend of mine, Brad Lea. He is a popular internet personality, and he was sharing about a time he was at a club and some men disrespected his wife. Most bros would think he needed to defend her honor no matter what. However, he talked about how he just ignored them and went home. I want everyone to understand that sometimes our ego will try to pick fights that our bodies can't manage. In the video, Brad made the wise point, saying, "What was the point of fighting these guys? So, they can kill me or put me in the hospital, and then nobody will be there for the next 50 years to take care of my wife and kids?" Between the Krav Maga training and this lesson from Brad, I realized that my job as a provider and a protector isn't to get into fights that I can avoid.

Of course, there are times when you'll need to fight. There will be times when you should not back down, where those you love need you to fight with everything you have. But there are many more times when you get cut off on the freeway and need to let it go. I don't want to blame this man or paint a picture of him being out of control. However, if we refuse to recognize that this man was probably experiencing the same kind of stress that you or I have felt, and simply made the wrong choice by acting on his frustrations, we risk allowing a similar incident to happen in our own lives. Someone reading this might learn a lesson that could potentially save their life. I know I've never made a wise decision when I'm caught up in the emotion of the moment.

One of the most important lessons I've learned over the last 10 years is to not react to the circumstances around me. When I have a bad moment, it's usually when I forget this lesson. In his amazing book *Man's Search for Meaning*, Victor Frankel says, "Between stimulus and response, there is a space. In that space is our power to choose our response. In our response lies our growth and our freedom." The man who survived will probably spend a good portion of his life in prison. Both men were probably having an off day, just needing to take a breath. Instead, this tragedy took place.

It's time to step up and lead as men, husbands, and fathers. No more acting out based on unregulated emotions. We need to be wise, heart-centered leaders who stand for honor and truth.

Top Five Things That Make a Man Attractive

Imposter syndrome will ruin your chances to be a king, own the room, and attract the lifestyle you crave. When you haven't healed from it, you'll overcompensate and will always try to prove that you're worthy. You end up looking like a dancing monkey and you're nothing but a try-hard. I did that for years. Bless my heart, but I would post so many things, just hoping people would see how amazing I was. What I was really saying was please love me, I'm worthy of knowing. But it was my blindspot—it was all subconscious.

In reality, it came off as "look at me, look how cool I think I am," and of course, it was putting people off. Once I made a shift, people noticed that I quit trying to prove myself. Now I know how nice it is when I don't have anything to prove. You can go to an event and just enjoy yourself, and not worry about how you're perceived. And naturally, people notice that too.

Social media made it very obvious those that were try-hards, and I'm as guilty as anyone. For example, I once posted a picture of me and my girlfriend at this under-the-ocean restaurant in the Maldives. What I was portraying was, "Look how amazing my life is. I'm eating at this restaurant. I've got this gorgeous date. . . ." Well, the truth behind that picture is that I forgot to get a reservation, so we had to get lunch instead of dinner. I booked way too many consecutive flights, and the girl I was with can't sleep on planes, so we hadn't slept in 48 hours.

Both of us were so tired, we just went back to the bungalow and fell asleep. We didn't wake up for almost 24 hours and missed our entire time in the Maldives. I booked another flight to go to Dubai to spend New Year's there, but by the time we landed in Dubai, we just wanted to be back in the Maldives. We were already on to the next adventure without even being able to enjoy the one we just had. As you'd expect, we fought the entire New Year's because we were so irritable, so Dubai was also a complete mess.

On paper, the whole thing looked like the trip of a lifetime. We were both miserable, but I was still posting as if we were having the times of our lives. If you were just watching my story, you'd think this guy has the greatest life ever. But I haven't even told the full story.

From the United States, we took a red-eye flight to London. But I didn't know she couldn't sleep on planes. She's a walking zombie to kick-off the trip and I had us booked on another red eye the next night to India so we can see the Taj Mahal. We landed in the city Agra, which is the third most polluted city in the world, and I forgot or never bothered to pay attention to the fact that she has asthma. Then, we get the insane experience of being driven around India to our hotel room. I thought I was gonna die at least 20 times.

When we finally got to the Taj Mahal, her asthma was so bad, she couldn't even get out of the car. We never got within 1,000 yards of the Taj Mahal, yet we got a picture. But because of the smog, you can barely see it in the background. We left there to have dinner at this epic Indian restaurant, but she didn't eat because she didn't like Indian food. The next night it was on to the Maldives and then Dubai, which we've covered. At this point, both of us are a total train wreck and are basically broken up.

I wish the story ended there, and you might think it's about to take a surprising romantic twist, especially when I tell you I booked a flight to Switzerland. My whole life, I wanted to ski the Matter-horn. Well, typical for me at the time, I didn't bother to ask her if she wanted to ski. Unbeknownst to me, she had a skiing accident the year before. As far as I knew, she used to be a big skier but the year before, she had a huge accident, woke up bloody and buried in snow. Needless to say, she wasn't ready to get back on the slopes.

But there we were on the Matterhorn, the nicest ski resort in Switzerland and maybe the world. Two days before, we were taking selfies on the beaches and in a bungalow in the Maldives. Through the lens of Instagram, it looked like the life, but really, the whole thing was a fucking disaster. I was posting every picture like it's the most beautiful trip. What I didn't post was that it took us three hours to get down the first bunny slope because she was so trauma-tized and exhausted.

Did we go home? No. We went to Paris. Seriously. We were both so bothered by each other that we just ended things there. We broke up in the city of love. It could have been the trip of a lifetime, had I bothered to find out one damn thing that mattered to her. What I should have done is found out what she wanted. The whole thing was about me so I could post all those pictures. I wanted peo-ple to see, and have photographic proof, that I was the world's great-est boyfriend. I wanted to prove how special my life was, but the truth was, I didn't enjoy any of it.

I've come a long way since then, and through the grace of God, I've let that desperate young boy, my inner child, know that he's more than enough. All toxic masculinity comes from an ignored or suppressed inner child. We'll get leaky with our sexual energy, we'll make reactive decisions, we'll be a bad friend, and we'll be an unconcerned romantic partner. We live in a world where those who are lifted up as kings are really attention-craving, greedy boys. The media lifts them up, but will just as quickly tear them apart.

If you want a glimpse at what toxic masculinity looks like, there are plenty of examples online. Too many men are predatory in nature and their energy is based on taking. Healthy masculinity is sacrificial in nature and must give. Healthy masculinity creates warriors who battle against the dark forces that enslave those to unhealthy desires and keep them from pursuing being a man of integrity. The opposite of toxic masculinity is heroic masculinity. It's all around us, and we all depend on it for our safety. This kind of masculinity is almost always taken for granted and is reviled now more than ever. However, when hardships come, healthy masculinity is required, even by the same people who have condemned it or claim to have it.

To be a king and lead people with a servant-heart, it means you must master these five things that will make you an attractive man:

1. **Be a Leader of Men.**
   - If you can effectively lead people, you'll gain friendships, vocational opportunities, and high-quality women will appreciate you for it.
2. **Be a Successful Risk-Taker.**
   - Women want to feel alive and fully feel emotions; they want to envision an adventurous, passionate life with you. The key word here is *successful.* Don't be boyish in your risks or you'll repel the same people you're trying to attract.
3. **Be a Protector of Loved Ones.**
   - This includes being physically, emotionally, and financially supportive to those you love and for those who love you. This doesn't mean allowing people to leech off you by being a people pleaser. No! Just the opposite. It's having the confidence to do what's needed to maintain safety.
4. **Be Emotionally Intelligent.**
   - People are going to test you, and women want to make sure you can't be moved by others. How do you handle stress? How do you grow from failure? This allows the woman to learn if she can trust you to hold strong so that

she can fully express her full feminine range—from rage to pleasure.

5. **Be Pre-Selected by Other Women.**
   - Women don't have time to vet every guy they run across. If a woman constantly sees you with other high-value women, she will assume you pass the other four things.

Be Appreciated

I had a member join my program, and he came up to me and said, "I want to tell you why I joined the group. I watched you walk into the gym one time, and you didn't know me, but I knew who you were from social media. You were by yourself, but you just had a grin from ear to ear the whole time. I was just watching you work out, and I could tell that you were legitimately happy and just enjoying this life." He was absolutely correct. It has taken time, and I've had my fair share of cringe moments and growing pains, but now I'm self-amused at the beauty and the ridiculousness of my own life.

That is a very underrated quality that I wish every man gets to experience at least once in his life. With this book, my program, my podcast, and everything else I'm doing, it's my mission that you get to feel that way every single day. Do you just enjoy yourself? Do you enjoy your own company without the need to distract yourself, talk to someone, or do something to feel seen?

Self-amusement is such a beautiful thing. I've come to realize, especially since gaining a bit of influence, that people always observe. People are always paying attention. Little kids are experts at this—they can instantly gauge if you're genuinely happy or on edge. It's all about the energy you exude. People either gravitate toward you or shy away. I've always aspired to be the kind of person whose arrival lifts the spirits of those around. Sadly, too many believe they can mask their true selves, but that artificial approach can't be hidden. True leaders understand that even in moments unseen, it's what they do and how they make others feel that truly counts.

Who are you when no one is looking? And who are you when everyone is looking? Do you change your tune? Do you shift your strut? Or are you so invested in living your life that no matter the circumstance, you're unapologetically yourself? That's what leadership is. That's what being a king is.

As I noted in Chapter 8, what every man wants is to be appreciated, and that starts with you. Look yourself in the eyes in the mirror every single morning and not turn away. You are worthy. View your true power and remain humble.

Be honest. Be in integrity. And be the king you were born to be.

10

Be Extraordinary

From FRUSTRATED to FULFILLED

"Ability is what you're capable of doing. Motivation determines what you do. Attitude determines how well you do it."

—Lou Holtz

THROUGHOUT THIS BOOK, I've written often about being extraordinary. If you're like me, that word brings ideas of swimming with sharks, running with the bulls in Spain, traveling to over 100 countries in less than 10 years, and being the best friend, son, daughter, boss, and human you can possibly be. But we need to redefine what *extraordinary* is.

My friend, the one from Chapter 7 who I left my Lake Powell trip to spontaneously go see, the man who felt like he was wrong for needing more intimacy, the father who co-parents his daughter and is a highly successful lawyer—he is an extraordinary man. He's not extraordinary because he always climbs mountain peaks, saves babies from burning buildings, or donates millions to charitable causes. He perfectly defines how an ordinary man living an ordinary life can offer so much love and authenticity to everyone around him and as a result, the entire world.

He's probably just like you. He's made mistakes, his mental and spiritual resilience is tested daily, and sometimes the voices that try to make him feel small, weak, and insecure seem more true than the beautiful, honorable, and powerful man he sees in the mirror. I'm just like him too. I have my moments (that sometimes turn into days) where I feel frustrated, stuck, and on-edge.

The core sense of frustration that most of us feel is not a bad thing. It's not something to be ashamed of nor is it something that will go away by distracting ourselves from it, suppressing it, or intellectualizing it away. All toxicity comes from signals ignored, intuition not trusted, energy misused, or actions done out of integrity. Sadly, most people become adjusted to this way of thinking, living, and behaving. That's not the kind of ordinary that anyone wants to be.

Showing up on time every time, being a compassionate parent, or being willing to stand for truth is what we all should associate with being ordinary. Being ordinary is nothing to be feared. What if every man embodied every single one of these chapters? What would the world be like, how much health would we have, and how much wealth would we be able to share with everyone if every man embodied complete and total integrity? What if being extraordinary was ordinary?

What Every Human Wants

Your level of spiritual development is what allows you to BE ONE with your true self. The pain caused by others will start to disappear the moment that all parts of your personality are recognized. This doesn't mean you won't ever feel pain, but that when you do, you won't be taken over by an aspect of yourself that's been hidden in the shadows. Only when you're free from shame and the suffering that comes from negative behaviors can you truly be at peace with yourself.

Clare W. Graves, the former Professor Emeritus of Psychology at Union College in New York, defined the psychological maturity of human beings and described consciousness in eight different areas. As we mature, we have to evolve to access all parts of ourselves. If we don't, our problems will continue to get worse until we fully grow into each area.

Here are the eight areas:

1. **Survivalistic** (Beige)
   - Theme: Do whatever you must to just stay alive.
   - Characteristics: Habitual, primal, animalistic, unconscious.
2. **Tribalistic** (Purple)
   - Theme: Follow others and obey what they say. You live for the betterment of the clan, and safety only comes from sticking together.
   - Characteristics: Simplistic, obedient, superstitious, magical.

3. **Egocentric** (Red)
   - Theme: Be who you are and do what you want, regardless of impact.
   - Characteristics: Selfishness, demanding, grandiose, aggressive.
4. **Purposeful** (Blue)
   - Theme: Life has predetermined outcomes, but it's your responsibility to live with meaning and direction.
   - Characteristics: Lawful, discipline, stability, authoritarian.
5. **Strategic** (Orange)
   - Theme: Play the game to win and do whatever you need to make things happen.
   - Characteristics: Analytical, achievement, self-focused.
6. **Egalitarian** (Green)
   - Theme: Seek peace within yourself, find community, and treat others with fairness.
   - Characteristics: Sensitivity, fairness, communal.
7. **Integrative** (Yellow)
   - Theme: Live fully and responsibly and learn to become one with all things.
   - Characteristics: Flexibility, surrender, aliveness, curiosity.
8. **Holistic** (Turquoise)
   - Theme: Experience the fullness of life through the unity of mind, body, and spirit.
   - Characteristics: Compassion, intuition, enlightenment.

You'll notice, the left side holds the more intense characteristics and are more individualistic. The ones on the right side are more community focused. These are all necessary levels of consciousness, yet you do not want to predominantly remain in those on the left side. If you do, it's a recipe for toxicity. It's best to live and be surrounded by those who are purposeful or holistic yet utilize strategic and integrative consciousness when getting things done. Also, we must be careful that we do not "slide" down the spiral when we

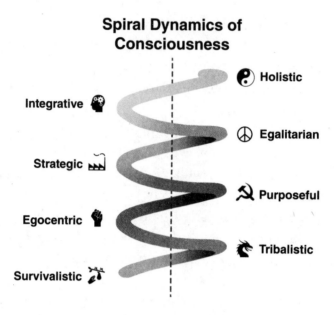

Spiral Dynamics of Consciousness

interact with someone in a lower level of consciousness. However, it is equally important to be able to effectively communicate with anyone regardless of where they are.

Each "leveling up" allows you to let go of things that no longer serve you. This is spiritual mastery, and this is what every human truly desires.

Tools for Spiritual Mastery

There are many tools and practices you can use to "spiral up" toward increased self-awareness. In the following, I've included a few to get you started. Not only can these practices help you access higher levels, but they can help stop you from sliding down in difficult times.

- Gratitude and Celebration
  o Celebrating and living with gratitude is how we best honor God. Everything can and should be a celebration.

- **Remember Your True Identity**
  - o Often, we don't know what the right answer is or what we should do. By accessing our true identity, we tap into the version of ourselves that would do things in the best way possible.
- **Plant Medicine**
  - o This is a powerful tool that is often used to help with trauma, addiction, and other disorders. It's also beneficial to help us break out of negative patterns or stuck places. One of the most important parts of using plants as medicine is understanding them and respecting their origins. Use them with care. This is not a tool for everyone and must be used with intention and integrity.
- **Breathwork**
  - o Breathwork is more than an exercise of breathing correctly or with intent. Breathing techniques can be used for major transformation and healing. Breathwork encompasses a broad range of whole-being therapeutic practices and exercises used to relieve mental, physical, and/or emotional tension.
- **Prayer and Meditation**
  - o Connection to God is fundamental to any authentic spiritual journey. Whether you refer to God as "the Father," "Universe," or "Source," use the term that resonates with you. Ultimately, we must learn to rely on and know that something bigger than ourselves is guiding us through all things.
- **Dance**
  - o When we celebrate and dance, happily and in a childlike state, we are honoring God with our freedom and joy. This is a great way to express our spirituality that most people only associate with partying or being intoxicated.

Having a Servant-Heart

Every morning I start my day with the same prayer: "God, please lead me to the people that I can help today." This prayer immediately changes my focus; instead of resisting beginning each day or looking at what I can gain from others, it helps me seek out those I can give to, knowing God is putting them in my path. That change in focus is everything. I follow it up with, "Give me the wisdom to know how to help and the courage to act on it."

This simple prayer is my way of reminding myself that who I strive to be is someone living for something much bigger than myself while simultaneously honoring myself, my needs, and my morals. If I pray for courage, God doesn't just hand it to me. I am given *opportunities* to be courageous. When I pray for patience, it's not given to me on a silver platter. I have to take a breath and be patient when someone cuts me off. When I prayed for presence, God didn't give it to me—I had to choose not to text and drive, releasing my fears around being unproductive.

Having a servant-heart is what will make you superhuman. It's what will shift your focus on how you can serve others, knowing and trusting in your ability to take care of yourself while also having the humility to receive love and support from others. The kind of love you should strive to embody is a combination of what the Greeks called philia and agape. *Philia* describes the bond seen in long-standing friendships. It is derived from the Greek term *phílos* meaning "that which is important and loved closely." *Agape* is the highest form of love and refers to the incomparable, immeasurable love that one can access. This represents unconditional and perfect love without blemish. By embodying both of these, you'll be a magnet for opportunities to be a healthy human, able to combat any toxicity within or around you.

How to Find and Define Your Purpose

Charity, being of service, and making positive contributions is how you leave a legacy for generations to come. Donating your time to support those around you is extremely beneficial for you and your community. It's statistically proven that people who volunteer regularly are healthier both physically and mentally. Individuals who have volunteered throughout their lifetime typically live longer and have better psychological well-being. In addition to the health benefits, volunteering gives people a sense of purpose. The fulfilling feeling of giving back and contributing to society is unparalleled.

Many people are given a sense of purpose via an organized religion. There are many benefits to being a part of one; however, just like faith without works is dead, so is religion without spirituality. God has given us so many forms and ways to reach our creator, yet it is through action that we do so. We have to meet God halfway.

"The purpose of my life is to share my tremendous love with all of God's children, bringing happiness to others through my playful soul and by being an example of living an extraordinary life." This is the mission statement for my life and my guiding force. It is the filter that I can run any idea or decision through to determine what I should do.

It took me years and being fully immersed for those six days at the Tony Robbins event to come up with it. It's not something I just came up with while on a hike, yet I believe that I can shed some light and provide a framework to define your own life purpose.

Here are the steps, as best as I can explain, on what the process looks like:

1. First, get crystal clear on what values you want to have at the front of your life. If you listen to mine, you can see that they are:
   - Love.
   - Happiness.
   - Playful.
   - Living Extraordinarily.

To figure out your values, first make a list of your top 20. Write everything that comes to mind without stopping. Then you need to prioritize them. Which one is first? Compare two against each other and whichever one feels better, move it up. Repeat this until they're in order and then focus on your top three to five.

2. Next, write down three things that you currently do that align with those top five values and three things that you want to do more of in the future to strengthen those values. Here's an example for my core value of love:

   - Spend time with my nieces and nephews and best friends' kids.
   - Gather with my friends and connect on a deep level.
   - Share my life through my podcast.
   - Go on walks with the men I coach.

   Once you've written out all your actions, you'll have a powerful vision that opens your eyes to your dream life.

3. Imagine there are no barriers and anything you wanted you could make happen. What would your life look like? Envision it, write it down, and feel the emotions as if it were happening right now.

4. The last step is to pretend you are a visitor attending your own funeral. Write out the speech that your spouse, one of your future kids, and/or a best friend would give at your funeral if you lived by your values and took action on everything you said for your entire life. How would they talk about you? What stories would they tell? What kind of emotion would they feel sharing their love for you?

This is the basis for creating your mission statement for your life, defining your purpose of being here on Earth. I suggest writing it out as what you hope to become, not necessarily what you are or how you see yourself right now. It's a guiding point and an identity you will work toward until you become exactly who you're meant to be.

Be Fulfilled

To be extraordinary, you have to dare to take risks. Taking risks is not limited to climbing Mt. Kilimanjaro, starting a podcast, or being in a rodeo (which I recently checked off my bucket list). I rode a beast of a bull for 2.7 seconds, just like Tim McGraw sang in "Live Like You Were Dying." But do you know what else is risky? Responding with care and compassion when someone is yelling at you, abusing you, or trying to make you feel small. Being vulnerable and risking being judged is one of the most extraordinary actions you can take. So is being honest and 100% authentic when your mind is screaming at you to deflect, lie, or change your tune. Doing the right thing when no one is watching is also a hallmark of being extraordinary.

Dare to be seen. Dare to make mistakes and own them when you do. Dare to ask for help and give it when someone asks you. Be there for your friends, become a leader among men, be a present father, and give your work your all, no matter if it's your dream job or just what pays the bills. Take action to be a good man and transform toxicity into personal triumph.

Conclusion

"Character, not circumstances, make the man."
—Booker T. Washington

Two DECADES AGO, I stumbled upon the book *Think and Grow Rich* by Napoleon Hill. Like so many entrepreneurs I know, it revolutionized my thinking. Among its wealth of insights, there's an entire chapter dedicated to the concept of "masterminds." Hill describes a mastermind as a "coordination of knowledge and effort, in a spirit of harmony, between two or more people, for the attainment of a definite purpose." This resonated with me, and I was keen on forming or joining a mastermind of my own.

In my early days as a real estate agent, I had the privilege to join my first genuine mastermind. Called Top Producers, it was orchestrated by Mike Ferry. These meetings were hugely transformative. Every quarter, we'd assemble in various locations. Only agents who sold 75 or more homes annually could participate. At these gatherings, we'd split into groups, sharing trade secrets and strategies that propelled us to the top. I recall being seated alongside industry greats like Brady Sandoval from Palm Springs, Utah's famed Joan Pate, and the standout agent from San Diego, Chris Heller. I was so inspired by Chris's methods that I adopted his system, which I still utilize. Interestingly, he later ascended to be the CEO of Keller Williams, leading it to become the largest real estate agent company in the country.

Throughout my journey, I've been a part of several other influential masterminds, such as The Avengers for real estate, Tony Robbins Platinum membership and the 100 Million Mastermind, where membership requires a staggering $100,000 annual fee. Every mastermind I've joined has yielded returns far exceeding my expectations. It's challenging to capture the essence of a mastermind's power in words. To truly comprehend it, you have to experience it firsthand. It's akin to trying to explain the feeling of true love to someone who's never experienced it.

In my own way, We Are The They is a kind of mastermind, albeit one unlike any I've ever seen or experienced. Within it, we employ a principle of multiplication. Hosting 50 individuals for three days doesn't just yield 50 relationships or 50 collective ideas. Each of the 50 participants brings their own network, resulting in an exponential 2,500 potential connections! This multiplicative effect is where the true magic lies.

Our quarterly mastermind events are called a "Ludus." Historically, a Ludus was a gladiator training school in ancient Rome, a place synonymous with training, play, and sport. This playful element is integral to our philosophy and is infused in every mastermind weekend. Playfulness, training, and education are vital for the outcomes we strive for.

For those tracking We Are The They and are curious to join, consider this your open invite. Engage with our community, participate in our leadership program, and make lasting connections. Dive into our app, chat with members, and even consider our annual adventure trips! At the time of writing this, over 70 men just went to Spain's iconic Running of the Bulls and next is hiking to the breathtaking Machu Picchu in Peru.

This isn't a pitch to join us. It's an invitation. Reach out to any of our 500+ legacy members and hear their testimonials. And even if you decide our mastermind isn't for you, I urge you to create or join one. Rally your peers, connect with those you admire, and harness the undeniable magic that only a mastermind can offer.

Living a Complete Life as a Man of Character

A legacy is leaving a lasting impact on the world. It's a gift passed down through generations: wisdom, insights, money, property, or maybe most importantly, stories. It can also be a business or the profits from a business, set up in a family trust, foundation, or charity. Leaving a legacy means dreaming big and changing the world for the better, and it is a powerful driver for the most successful people on the planet.

Many men initially sense they want to leave a mark through their work, but they don't know how to do so. To truly make a lasting impression, you must first answer a pivotal question: what does it mean, to you, to leave a legacy?

Much like integrity, a legacy is self-defined. Not by religion or society. I'll give you an insight that took me years to realize: The depth, breath, and potency of your personal integrity is what will determine the power, longevity, and beauty of your legacy.

You may be a kick-ass parent or you're just now awakening to the magnitude of the divine role you have as a steward of someone else's life. You may know the magic and wisdom in tithing, or you may just now realize that the best way to keep what you have is to give it all away. You may have a business that does something good, true, and beautiful for the world, or you may be realizing your means of wealth creation come at a harmful expense to those less fortunate.

Regardless, it's your duty as a man of character to transform your life into complete integrity—via the kind of people you associate with, your depth of presence to your loved ones, and how close you truly are to living your life surrendered to God's will.

Here's a fact of life: There's nothing like a strong and diverse community that will keep you humble and in check. Community is the key to being of service and being able to be served. Imagine your life surrounded by hundreds of people you *know* have got your back, won't try anything icky with your loved ones, and will fuel you to greatness in every area of life.

Conclusion to the Conclusion . . . Which Is Where It All Begins

The great philosopher Plato was once asked what surprises him the most about human beings, his answer: "They get bored in childhood, and they hurry to grow up, but then they miss their childhood. They lose their health to earn money, but they pay money to regain their health. Worried about tomorrow they forget about today. In the end, they neither live today nor tomorrow. They live as if they'll never die, but they die as if they never lived."

By itself, this book can't do anything to change your life. If you don't put the effort in, there's very little that you'll get out of it. Like anything in life, we get out of it what we put in. I've done my best, employed the best book producer and editor, and partnered with the best publisher to create the guidebook for you to make the changes you need. I am confident in what this will do for you and your family. But only you will be able to affect the direction and outcome of your life.

By reading this book, you've joined a global family and a revolutionary movement. It's an honor to be a part of it with you. The basis of that movement is a high standard and a striving to be a good man. If you agree that you're here on this planet at this specific time in history, to do exactly what you must to BE ONE, I offer you this standard:

1. I will not talk negatively about anyone, present or not. If I have an issue with someone, I agree to honor them and those connected to them by speaking respectfully.
2. I agree to show up for others. We all have busy lives, but I will be there for those who need me. This goes for all my personal and professional relationships.
3. I agree to never embarrass others or myself with illegal or immoral behavior, especially toward women and children. I maintain a zero-tolerance policy for any such behavior.

This life is a gift; don't waste it.

Now you know what it means to be a good man, so go, BE ONE.

About the Author

Jimmy Rex is no stranger to the pursuit of an extraordinary life. He's the innovative mind behind We Are The They (WATT), the groundbreaking global coaching program and social movement, helping men everywhere lead truly exceptional lives. The resonance of his influence doesn't end there. Many know and love him as the host of "The Jimmy Rex Show," a podcast and touchstone for inspiration-seekers far and wide. Alongside his best-selling work, *You End Up Where You're Heading*, his newest offering, *BE ONE: How to Be a Healthy Man in Toxic Times*, is a game-changing narrative of masculinity, giving men—and the women and teens in their lives—the tools to not just survive but truly thrive.

Before his pivot to transformative coaching and authorship, Jimmy made waves in the real estate sector. Over two decades, he personally sold more than 2,500 homes, while also leading his team to an additional 4,000 homes sold to eager investors. Beyond this, his entrepreneurial spirit saw him invest in and establish over 20 diverse companies and 15 delectable restaurants.

Beyond his successes in real estate and the entrepreneurial world, Jimmy is an avid adventurer. From daring feats like swimming with tiger sharks and conquering the heights of Mount Kilimanjaro, to heartfelt humanitarian missions, such as undercover operations to rescue children from sex trafficking, his drive to experience and improve the world knows no bounds. His travels have taken him to over 106 countries as of the writing of this book.

Jimmy's commitment to positive change is evident in everything he does. As he continues to inspire and guide countless individuals, he remains steadfast in his mission: to share immeasurable love and illuminate the path to an extraordinary life.

Index